海外视角商务汉语教材系列

中国国家对外汉语教学领导小组办公室规划教材
Project of NOTCFL of the People's Republic of China

Hanban

Textbook

II

A BUSINESS TRIP TO CHINA

Xiaojun Wang Ph. D.

张旺熹　孙德金

Conversation & Application

基础商务汉语 下
会话与应用

北京语言大学出版社
BEIJING LANGUAGE AND CULTURE
UNIVERSITY PRESS

Printed in China
中国国家汉办赠送
Donated by Hanban, China

图书在版编目（CIP）数据

基础商务汉语：会话与应用.下册.Textbook & Workbook=A Business Trip To China:
Conversation & Application /(美)王晓钧，张旺熹，孙德金编著.—北京：
北京语言大学出版社，2009重印
　ISBN 978-7-5619-1524-0

　Ⅰ.基… Ⅱ.①王…②张…③孙… Ⅲ.商务－汉语－口语－对外汉语教学－教材
Ⅳ.H195.4

　中国版本图书馆CIP数据核字(2005)第126614号

书　　　　名：	**基础商务汉语**：会话与应用（下册）
责任印制：	陈辉

出版发行：	北京语言大学出版社
社　　　址：	北京市海淀区学院路15号　　邮政编码：100083
网　　　址：	http://www.blcup.com
电　　　话：	发行部 82303648/3591/3651
	编辑部 82303647
	读者服务部 82303653/3592
	网上订购电话 82303668
	客户服务信箱 service@blcup.net
印　　　刷：	北京新丰印刷厂
经　　　销：	全国新华书店

版　　　次：	2005年11月第1版　　2009年9月第3次印刷
开　　　本：	889毫米×1194毫米　1/16　印张：19.25
字　　　数：	197千字　印数：6001-9000
书　　　号：	ISBN 978-7-5619-1524-0/H·05138

07200（全套）（随书赠CD一张）

凡有印装质量问题，本社出版部负责调换。电话：82303590

Contents

Preface 序

Timothy Light
黎天睦

I was very honored when Professor Wang Xiaojun asked me to write a preface to his excellent textbook. A highly successful teacher, an effective department administrator and leader, and a very accomplished scholar in applied linguistics and teaching materials, Professor Wang, as always, makes a significant contribution to the field with this much needed material. His natural gifts for leading are also evident, as he has been assisted in this project by five others. Anyone who has attempted to write a textbook with several other people knows the daunting challenges presented by the number. That the product has emerged so successfully is a credit to all of the participants.

I wish that there had been textbooks such as this one when I first began to study Chinese in the mid 1960's. Available to us in the United States at that time were oral texts for the beginning level that were based on grammar manipulation exercises and reading texts that were valued on the basis of the number of characters that one could learn in the shortest amount of time. Beyond the beginning level, classes in the United States tended not to branch too far beyond decoding and translation. (Not surprisingly, classes in Hong Kong and Taiwan were a good deal more interactive and demanding even then.) I also wish that there had been more widely available materials for studying Chinese for special purposes, such as a possible career in business. The Mandarin Center, the Taipei Language Institute, the Stanford Center (all in Taiwan) and the New Asia—Yale-in-China Chinese Language Centre at the Chinese University of Hong Kong all produced fine specially focused materials for use within their own walls. But American students studying at home were left largely in the dark that there were such things and so did not imagine there was a possibility of formally learning specialized vocabulary and discourse formats.

How far we have come is exemplified by *A Business Trip to China—Conversation & Application.* Notably interactive, these materials introduce vocabulary that is fundamental to business and provide useful and relevant dialogues and exercises to practice that vocabulary and the linguistic-cultural conventions for using that vocabulary in business situations. The authors have been imaginative and thoughtful in the situations which they have selected for the bases of the dialogues and accompanying exercises. They have been comprehensive in including practice with typical forms that business people must fill out during the course of their working day.

Going to a country to work when one has at one's command only a general knowledge of basic language is frequently quite disorienting. One can get along to a degree in the simplest of daily tasks and can negotiate transport and lodging and order a meal, but often even the most elementary tasks of one's professional life are simply out of reach. The fortunate students who study this book have before them the happy prospect of having a significant jump ahead of their predecessors when they arrive in China and begin to get to work.

The authors collectively—and especially Professor Wang are to be thanked for this contribution to the advancement of the students of Chinese.

To the Users

A *Business Trip to China — Conversation & Application I and II* are designed for learners at a pre-intermediate level who have learned basic Chinese in a variety of settings. They are English speakers, or are using English as their principal second language, and they are interested in having a career or doing business among Chinese speaking communities.

At the outset of the twenty-first century, Chinese is spoken by over 1.3 billion people — more than any other language. The demand for Chinese language instruction is therefore increasing rapidly. There is, however, a lack of suitable teaching materials for English speakers wanting to learn Chinese for business communication. Although some textbooks of business Chinese have recently been published in the USA and China, these materials tend to be designed for students who have studied Chinese for at least three years or more. Very often, the contents of these texts are quite complicated and use many uncommon business terms.

Students at overseas universities, with varying language backgrounds, often desire instruction in aspects of real world Chinese business language and culture. To provide a practical, motivating, and user-friendly business Chinese textbook, we have employed the following pedagogical approaches to meet the needs of both instructors and students:

■ A communicative approach: We believe that the fundamental goal of these textbooks is to improve learners' business Chinese communication abilities. For this purpose, the lessons in the textbooks feature a series of business conversations portraying a Western businessman's business trip to China. We have tried to make these conversations short and interesting in order to motivate students to "role play" and thus be able to memorize large portions of them. We have also carefully selected frequently used words and terms, especially business vocabulary featured from our statistical research, and "recycled" them throughout the conversations. In order to encourage students to speak using the target language without looking at the text, we have provided a series of pictures after each workbook lesson, thus encouraging students to speak out using the new vocabulary and sentence structures.

■ An integrated approach: To communicate with Chinese speakers in a business environment, not only are language skills required, but also a knowledge of Chinese business culture and economic information. Therefore, unlike most Chinese textbooks, we have included two components in addition to the textbook's language component — Chinese business culture and economic information. To introduce the culture in a more interesting and engaging way, David — the American businessman who goes to China for the first time, narrates his own stories, including his personal experiences and culture shocks in the form of a diary. The "Economic Information" sections, included after each lesson, are introduced visually with concise tables and in plain English. We also believe that the four language skills — listening, speaking, reading and writing, are related to each other, even though they can be acquired at different paces. It is our goal to integrate the training of the four skills by designing a large number of exercises, many of which incorporate authentic materials.

■ An interactive approach: In order to provide a textbook that can meet most learners' needs, we have made the business Chinese easy enough for pre-intermediate students to get started, but also challenging enough to allow students of varying language experience to group together and learn from each other. Therefore, students will not have to wait to learn professional level language and usages until they reach an advanced level. In both the textbooks and workbooks, we have many communicative activities designed to foster interaction among students as well as between teachers and students. These activities include dialogues, questions and answers, group activities, and role-plays. We also believe that students should master basic sentence structures and be able to generate new sentences while emphasizing communicative functions. In order to present grammatical training in a communicative manner, we have not only given concise explanations based on the features of each sentence structure, but also a basic format of the structure and examples of usage. In addition, we have provided substitutive drills as often as possible, and used or relycled the relevant vocabulary in those examples and drills.

In an effort to be user-friendly, this textbook series is divided into two parts (I & II), with each part having two volumes — a textbook and a workbook. According to a typical university curriculum, it will normally take one semester to cover each part of the course. Each lesson in the textbook includes two dialogues, grammar and sentence pattern drills, a diary in English comparing Chinese and Western business culture, concise economic information, and supplementary bilingual business words presented with tables. Each dialogue is given in both simplified and traditional characters with the associated *Pinyin* and English translations. The workbooks are designed to complement the textbooks. For the students' convenience, each section in the workbooks provides the vocabulary list for each dialogue appearing in the textbook. The various exercises (10 to 11 different kinds in each section) are based on communicative and interactive approaches with the focus on business conversation and applications. It is expected that instructors' preparation time will be saved while still meeting the various needs of students. The listening exercises should be used in conjunction with the accompanying CD. Appendices and bilingual vocabulary indices are also included in each book.

《基础商务汉语——会话与应用》系列教材可供具有初级汉语水平以上的学习者使用。凡是以英语为母语或主要交流语言并有兴趣在中国及华人社区从事商务活动的人，都可使用本教材来提高商务汉语的交际能力。

在 21 世纪之初，以汉语为母语的人口已达到 13 亿，其数量超过了世界上其他任何一种语言。汉语热也迅速升温。但是，很多以英语为媒介语的学习者却难以找到适合他们使用的商务汉语教材。虽然这样的教材近年来在中国和国外都出版过一些，但是往往要求学习者具备三年以上的日常汉语训练后才能涉猎，其课文内容的冗长复杂和专业词汇的生僻晦涩常常使初学者望而生畏。国外高校的汉语学生尽管有着不同的语言文化背景，但是他们都渴求学习到中国商务活动中真实的语言和文化。为了给学习者提供一部实用方便而又生动有趣的入门教材，我们在教学法上进行了下列的探索和创新，以满足师生的需要。

■ 突出交际能力的训练：我们深信商务汉语教学基本的和最终的目的都是提高学习者在商务活动中的交际能力。因此，这套教材的课文内容跟随一位西方商人的中国之行一步步展开。与此同时，我们尽量使每课的对话简短真切而又生动有趣，以便鼓励学生进入角色，进而能够记住大部分内容。我们也在词频统计的基础上仔细地选取使用频率较高的词汇，尤其是商业词汇，并尽量增加这些高频词在对话和练习中的重现率。为了鼓励学生用学到的商务汉语自由进行交际，我们还在练习册每课的后面提供了连环图片，学习者可根据图片的情节线索尝试使用新学到的词语和句型。

■ 加强综合技能的培养：在中国或以华人为主的商务氛围中进行交流，不仅要求有汉语技能，同时也需要具备一定的商业文化知识和对当地经贸情况的了解。有鉴于此，本教材有别于大多数语言教材的地方是，除了语言这一要素之外，还添加了另外两个要素——中国的商业文化和经贸信息。为了使学习者对中国商务文化有身临其境的感受，美国商人大卫用日记体的形式分段扼要地讲述了他第一次到中国经商的切身体会和感悟到的文化差异。每课正文之后我们还采用图表和简明的英语介绍相关的商业信息。在语言方面，我们也强调综合能力的训练。我们认为，语言的听、说、读、写四种能力是相辅相成的，但不必同步发展。为此，我们设计并提供了大量的仿真练习以提高学习者综合的语言能力。

■ 提倡互动式教学：为了满足绝大多数学习者的需要，我们的教材一方面尽量化难为易，使具备初级汉语水平的学生就可开始学习商务汉语；另一方面则带有一定伸缩性和挑战性，以利于不同程度的学习者结成语言伙伴，互相学习，取长补短。这样，学生就可以根据自己的需要，早日选择学习的方向，而不必等到学完高年级日常汉语之后才接触职业汉语。在相互配合的课本和综合练习册中，我们设计了很多交际练习以鼓励学习者之间和师生之间的互动交流。这些活动包括对话、问答、分组活动、模拟角色等等。在突出交际能力训练的同时，我们也意识到学习者必须掌握基本句型及类推以生成新句子的能力。为了达到在商务交际活动中进行语法训练的目的，我们不仅根据每个句型的特点作了针对性的说明，而且提供了基本的句式和用例，并引导学生运用新学到的词语做大量的句型操练，以建立语言接受能力和生成能力的互动。

基于方便教学者使用的目的，本教材分为上下两册，每册包括课本和综合练习两个分册。根据比较常见的国外大学的课程安排，每册教材一般可供一个学期使用。课本中的每一课都包括两段对话、相关的句型、注释和替换练习，以及日记体的中外商务文化比较和简要的经贸信息。为了扩大学习者的词汇量且便于查阅参考，每课还有汉英对照的用图表分类列出的常用商务词汇。每段对话都有简体字、繁体字、汉语拼音和英文翻译的相互对照，以便于学习者根据自己的情况选择和参考。综合练习册配合课本的内容而设计。为了学习者的便利，练习册中每课都提供了与课文中每个对话对应的词汇表。为每课设计的各种不同的练习都以功能教学和互动教学理念为指导，注重商务汉语会话和商务汉语应用能力的训练。我们希望这些教学材料在满足学生需要的同时，也能够节省教师的备课时间。此外，每册教材还附有与课文和练习配套的 CD 光盘，以及各类附录和双语词汇索引。

Abbreviations for Parts of Speech

Adj.	Adjective
Adv.	Adverb
AP	Adjective Phrase
AV	Auxiliary Verb
CE	Common Expression
Collo.	Colloquial
Conj.	Conjunction
Exc.	Exclamation
IE	Idiomatic Expression
Interj.	Interjection
Loc.	Localizer
MW	Measure Word
N	Noun
NP	Noun Phrase
Num.	Numerals
Obj.	Object
P	Particle
PN	Proper Noun
Pol.	Polite Expression
Prep.	Preposition
Pron.	Pronoun
PW	Place Word
QW	Question Word
Subj.	Subject
TW	Time Word
V	Verb
VP	Verb Phrase

第七课　小本生意
Lesson 7　Small Businesses

Dialogue 1　Strolling around the Streets ｜ 逛街

1

一、逛 街

玛　丽：我们今天的行程有半天空闲，要不要上街逛
　　　　逛？

大　卫：好主意！我也想借机了解一下这里的自由市场，
　　　　看看有哪些热门商品值得投资。

玛　丽：听说现在中国人的收入增加，生活水平也提高
　　　　了很多，那些经营小本生意的叫"个体户"，
　　　　要是生意做得好，钱赚得比工薪阶层还多呢！

大　卫：个体经营可以节省工资，老板也用不着给雇员
　　　　分红了，难怪有些国营职工自动下海了。

玛　丽：是啊。别再说了，我们还是赶快出门上街看看
　　　　吧。

大　卫：你看看，讲到逛街，你们女人就特别感兴趣。

Pinyin

Duìhuà I   Guàng Jiē

Mǎlì: Wǒmen jīntiān de xíngchéng yǒu bàntiān kòngxián, yào bu yào shàngjiē guàngguang?

Dàwèi: Hǎo zhǔyi! Wǒ yě xiǎng jièjī liǎojiě yíxià zhèli de zìyóu shìchǎng, kànkan yǒu nǎxiē rèmén shāngpǐn zhíde tóuzī.

Mǎlì: Tīng shuō xiànzài Zhōngguórén de shōurù zēngjiā, shēnghuó shuǐpíng yě tígāo le hěn duō, nàxiē jīngyíng xiǎoběn shēngyi de jiào "gètǐhù", yàoshi shēngyi zuò de hǎo, qián zhuàn de bǐ gōngxīn jiēcéng hái duō ne!

Dàwèi: Gètǐ jīngyíng kěyǐ jiéshěng gōngzī, lǎobǎn yě yòng bu zháo gěi gùyuán fēnhóng le, nánguài yǒuxiē guóyíng zhígōng zìdòng xiàhǎi le.

Mǎlì: Shì a. Bié zài shuō le, wǒmen háishì gǎnkuài chūmén shàngjiē kànkan ba.

Dàwèi: Nǐ kànkan, jiǎngdào guàngjiē, nǐmen nǚrén jiù tèbié gǎn xìngqu.

一、逛　街

瑪　麗：我們今天的行程有半天空閑，要不要上街逛
　　　　逛？

大　衛：好主意！我也想借機了解一下這里的自由市場，
　　　　看看有哪些熱門商品值得投資。

瑪　麗：聽說現在中國人的收入增加，生活水平也提高
　　　　了很多，那些經營小本生意的叫"個體户"，
　　　　要是生意做得好，錢賺得比工薪階層還多呢！

大　衛：個體經營可以節省工資，老板也用不着給雇員
　　　　分紅了，難怪有些國營職工自動下海了。

瑪　麗：是啊。別再說了，我們還是趕快出門上街看看
　　　　吧。

大　衛：你看看，講到逛街，你們女人就特別感興趣。

ENGLISH TEXT

Dialogue Ⅰ   Strolling around the Streets

Mary: We have half a day of free time in our schedule. Would you like to stroll around the streets?

David: Good idea! I would also like to take this opportunity to know more about the free market here. We can take a look and see what products are in high demand and worth investing in.

Mary: I heard that Chinese people's income has been increasing lately, and that their living standard has also increased a lot. Those who run small businesses are called "individual business owners". If business is good, they can earn more money than those who have regular jobs.

David: Running a business by oneself can save wages, and the boss doesn't need to share profits with his employee. No wonder some government workers and staff have voluntarily quit their jobs and engaged in trade.

Mary: Yeah. We should stop talking. We had better go out and start strolling around.

David: See! Whenever shopping and strolling around the streets is mentioned, you women get so excited!

 Notes

▶ Grammar & Pattern Drills

1. 值得 （V） "worth"

It is used to describe something which is worthwhile or worth doing. 值得 can be followed by a verb phrase or a clause. It can also be modified by an adverb.

Subj. + (Adv.) + 值得 + VP/Clause

Examples：

1. 这本书值得看。

   This book is worth reading.

2. 这个东西值得买下来。

   This is something worth buying.

Substitutive drills：

信用卡很方便，		申请。
笔记本电脑很有用，		买。
这家公司很大，	值得	你去看看。
卖方的报价不高，		我们考虑。
挣钱太少，不		干。

2. 叫 （V） "call; be called"

叫, literally meaning "to shout", can be used in several ways. However, 叫 here means "to be called". It must have one or two nouns or pronouns as its objects.

$$\text{Subj.} + \text{叫} + \text{Obj.}_1 + (\text{Obj.}_2)$$

Examples:

1. 你叫什么？

   What is your name? / What do you like to be called?

2. 玛丽叫大卫"大老板"。

   Mary calls David "big boss".

Substitutive drills:

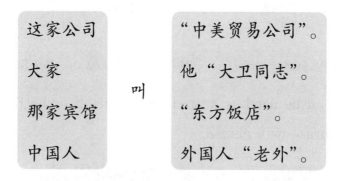

这家公司		"中美贸易公司"。
大家		他"大卫同志"。
那家宾馆	叫	"东方饭店"。
中国人		外国人"老外"。

3. 比 （Prep.） "than; compare with"

To express a comparison, 比 is used between two items being compared, and is usually followed by an adjectival phrase. Sometimes, the adjective may be modified by adverbial phrases.

$$A + 比 + B + (Adv.) + Adj. + (Adv.)$$

Examples：

1. 这个产品比那个更好。

   This product is even better than that one.

2. 他的收入比老板还多。

   His income is even more than that of the boss.

Substitutive drills：

今年的利润	去年	好。
零售商的回扣	批发商	高多了。
这些新产品	名牌货	还好。
个体户赚钱	国营职工	多。

（中间竖排：比）

4. 用不着 (V + Complement) "not need; have no use for"

This phrase can be used as a predicate by itself or be followed by a verb phrase, a noun phrase or a clause.

$$(Subj.) + 用不着 + (VP/NP/Clause)$$

Examples：

1. 他用不着说，我就知道了。

   He doesn't have to say it. I just know it.

2. 我有人民币，你用不着带信用卡了。

I have RMB，and you don't have to bring the credit card.

Substitutive drills：

今天天气不热，		开空调。
我在北京只住几天，		开银行账户。
你给我发电子邮件就好，	用不着	来公司。
打电话很方便，		传真。

5. 难怪 (Adv.) "no wonder"

It is used to connect two clauses，of which one is the reason of the other one. It is used when the relation between the cause and the result is obvious. 难怪 can be used either in the first clause or in the second one to show "the realization of the truth".

Examples：

1. 难怪他要去自由市场，那里的商品又好又便宜。

No wonder he wants to go to the free market；the products there are good and inexpensive.

2. 他卖的东西太贵了，难怪没人买。

The things he sells are too expensive. No wonder nobody wants to buy them.

Substitutive drills：

A.

难怪 | 有的国营职工下海了，没有销路， | 个体户赚钱多。这些产品太差了。

B.

他们做了很多广告，这是名牌， | 难怪 | 生意好。价钱高。

---

6. 还是……吧 (Adv. ... P) *expressing a preference for an alternative*

The thing preferred immediately follows 还是 as bias towards. 吧 is used as a modal particle tagged to commands，suggestions，or requests at the end of a sentence.

Examples：

1. 我们还是早点回家吧。

   We'd better go home earlier.

2. 还是你开车吧，安全一点儿。

   It will be better if you drive.

Substitutive drills：

我们		买名牌	
你们		去国营商场看看	
请他们	还是	先看看商品	吧。
去逛街		找李小姐	

Supplementary Vocabulary

中国的各类市场
Various Markets in China

表15

English	Chinese	*Pinyin*
state-operated market	国营商场	guóyíng shāngchǎng
free market	自由市场	zìyóu shìchǎng
a market of farm produce (in urban areas)	农贸市场	nóngmào shìchǎng
department store	百货商场	bǎihuò shāngchǎng
supermarket	超级市场/超市	chāojí shìchǎng/ chāoshì
night market	夜市	yèshì
morning market	早市	zǎoshì
country fair; market	集市	jíshì
(temple) fair	庙会	miàohuì
flea market	旧货市场	jiùhuò shìchǎng

Dialogue 2　Vendor's Stands

小　摊　儿

 二、小 摊 儿

老　板：您要买什么？我这个摊儿上什么都有。

玛　丽：我想买一些中国的布料，还想给朋友买点纪念品。

老　板：我的货物美价廉，随便挑。

大　卫：这个小古董不错，多少钱？可以打折吗？

老　板：没问题。要是质量有问题，我还保证退款。

玛　丽：我喜欢这块布料，可是太贵了，能不能便宜一点儿？

老　板：您就别讨价还价了，这可是高档货啊！

大　卫：我们想买一些布料带回美国去。可以订货吗？

老　板：当然可以，只要先付定金就行了。这些布料要是卖到美国去，您一定赚大钱！

玛　丽：可以用支票吗？

老　板：不行，得用现金，一手交钱，一手交货。

Pinyin

Duìhuà Ⅱ   Xiǎotānr

Lǎobǎn： Nín yào mǎi shénme? Wǒ zhège tānr shang shénme dōu yǒu.

Mǎlì： Wǒ xiǎng mǎi yìxiē Zhōngguó de bùliào, hái xiǎng gěi péngyou mǎi diǎn jìniànpǐn.

Lǎobǎn： Wǒ de huò wù měi jià lián, suíbiàn tiāo.

Dàwèi： Zhège xiǎo gǔdǒng búcuò, duōshao qián? Kěyǐ dǎzhé ma?

Lǎobǎn： Méi wèntí. Yàoshi zhìliàng yǒu wèntí, wǒ hái bǎozhèng tuìkuǎn.

Mǎlì： Wǒ xǐhuan zhè kuài bùliào, kěshì tài guì le, néng bu néng piányi yìdiǎnr?

Lǎobǎn： Nín jiù bié tǎo jià huán jià le, zhè kě shì gāodànghuò a!

Dàwèi： Wǒmen xiǎng mǎi yìxiē bùliào dàihuí Měiguó qu. Kěyǐ dìnghuò ma?

Lǎobǎn： Dāngrán kěyǐ, zhǐyào xiān fù dìngjīn jiù xíng le. Zhè xiē bùliào yàoshi màidào Měiguó qu, nín yídìng zhuàn dà qián!

Mǎlì： Kěyǐ yòng zhīpiào ma?

Lǎobǎn： Bù xíng, děi yòng xiànjīn, yì shǒu jiāo qián, yì shǒu jiāo huò.

二、小攤兒

老　闆：您要買什麼？我這個攤兒上什麼都有。

瑪　麗：我想買一些中國的布料，還想給朋友買點紀念品。

老　闆：我的貨物美價廉，隨便挑。

大　衛：這個小古董不錯，多少錢？可以打折嗎？

老　闆：沒問題。要是質量有問題，我還保證退款。

瑪　麗：我喜歡這塊布料，可是太貴了，能不能便宜一點兒？

老　闆：您就別討價還價了，這可是高檔貨啊！

大　衛：我們想買一些布料帶回美國去。可以訂貨嗎？

老　闆：當然可以，只要先付定金就行了。這些布料要是賣到美國去，您一定賺大錢！

瑪　麗：可以用支票嗎？

老　闆：不行，得用現金，一手交錢，一手交貨。

ENGLISH TEXT

Dialogue II   Vendor's Stands

Owner: Looking for anything specific? We have everything at this stand.

Mary: I would like to buy some Chinese fabrics and also some souvenirs for friends.

Owner: All my goods are good but inexpensive. Please choose anything as you like.

David: This small antique is not bad. How much is it? Are you going to give us a discount?

Owner: No problem. And if there is something wrong with the quality, I guarantee a refund.

Mary: I like this fabric, but it's too expensive. Can you reduce the price?

Owner: Please don't bargain with me on it. It is high-grade fabric indeed.

David: I would like to ship some fabrics back to the USA. Can I place an order?

Owner: Sure. You just have to pay the deposit first. If you take these fabrics to the USA, you will definitely make a big fortune.

Mary: Do you take checks?

Owner: No. We only accept cash. You hand me cash and I'll give you the goods.

 Notes

▶ Grammar & Pattern Drills

1. 什么 + …… + 都 …… （Pron. + Adv.） "any; whichever; whatever"

To express all-inclusion，什么 can be used by itself or followed by a noun with 都 to indicate whatever，whoever，wherever，etc.

Subj. + 什么 + (N) + 都 + V/Adj.

Examples：

1. 我什么外币都没有。

   I don't have any foreign currency.

2. 你什么时间来找我都可以。

   You can come to see me at any time.

Substitutive drills：

我		东西	不想买。
她		商场	想逛。
这家商店	什么	进口货	都 有。
张经理		人	遇到过。

2. 随便 （V/Conj.） "do as one please"

随便 can be followed by a noun, a verb or a clause to mean "to do as one likes". The subject is often left out.

(Subj.) +随便+······

Examples：

1. 请随便看。

   Please look around as you like.

2. 菜很多，随便吃。

   There is a lot of food. Help yourself.

Substitutive drills：

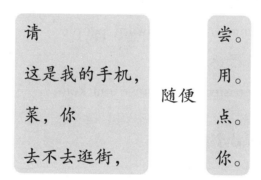

请		尝。
这是我的手机，	随便	用。
菜，你		点。
去不去逛街，		你。

3. 打折 （VP） "give a discount"

When talking about a discount, Chinese and English are different. In English, the emphasis is on the portion of the money which is not collected, e.g. 10% off, 20% off or 25% off, etc. In Chinese, however, the emphasis is on the amount of money which is actually collected. Therefore, 打九折

means that the cost is 90% of the original price. 八折 means 20% off. 七五折 means 25% off. 五折 or 对折 means 50% of the original price. The percentage of the original price is inserted between 打 and 折.

4. 对 (Prep.) "to; toward"

对 here is followed by a noun or noun phrase to make a prepositional phrase，and this phrase is placed before a verb or an adjective phrase to express attitude or frame of mind towards someone or something.

$$Subj. + 对 + N + VP/AP$$

Examples：

1. 王先生对人很友善。

   Mr. Wang is very friendly toward people.

2. 他对中国市场很感兴趣。

   He is very interested in Chinese markets.

Substitutive drills：

大卫		自由市场		特别感兴趣。
王老板		美国商品		很了解。
张经理	对	个体户的情况		知道得很少。
李小姐		高档货		没有兴趣。

5. 一点儿 (MW) **"a bit; slightly"**

In general，一点儿 means small quantities or low degree. It can also soften the tone. It is used either adverbially after a verb or an adjective，or attributively before a noun.

Examples：

1. 这个东西贵了一点儿。

   This thing costs a little too much.

2. 他有一点儿日元。

   He has a small amount of Japanese yen.

Substitutive drills：

A.

报价太高了，能不能低	
您订货太少，最好增加	一点儿。
美国人比较高大，衣服规格要大	

B.

他想在中国买		古董。
大卫在银行兑换了	一点儿	人民币。
玛丽在自由市场买了		纪念品。

6. 只要……就 (Conj. …Adv.) "only if...then...; as long as...then..."

只要……就 is used as a pair to form a conditional sentence. 只要 is movable. It may be placed before or after the subject. 只要 is usually used correlatively with 就 to mean "as long as" and 就 connects the result.

$$(Subj._1) + 只要…… + (Subj._2) + 就……$$

Examples:

1. 只要你诚信，生意就会好。

   Your business will get better as long as you stick to the principle of good faith.

2. 你只要答应这个条件，我就帮你的忙。

   As long as you accept this term, I will help you.

Substitutive drills:

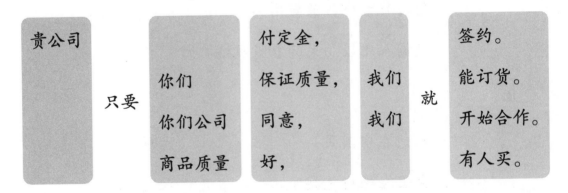

贵公司	只要	你们 你们公司 商品质量	付定金， 保证质量， 同意， 好，	我们 我们	就	签约。 能订货。 开始合作。 有人买。

Supplementary Vocabulary

十进制的数字表达
Digit Expressions of the Decimal System

表16

English	Chinese	Pinyin
one（single-digit）	个	gè
ten（double-digit）	十	shí
a hundred	百	bǎi
a thousand	千	qiān
ten thousand	万	wàn
a hundred thousand	十万	shí wàn
a million	百万	bǎiwàn
ten million	千万	qiān wàn
a hundred million	亿	yì
a billion	十亿	shí yì

David's Diary

Day 6: The Market System in China

A Free Market Economy

Being here makes me aware that China has embraced many aspects of capitalism and the free market. The Chinese government, with its political stand, maintains an overall socialist atmosphere while the burgeoning free market creates pockets of unrestraint. In fact, many Chinese people and some foreigners enjoy the free market very much, since not only can they have a large selection of merchandise from all over the world, but also often bargain for a lower price. I also see this situation in the crazy traffic around Beijing. When a traffic cop is present, everyone follows the law. However, when no policemen are around, some drivers don't even stop at traffic lights! I heard that the traffic is getting better recently due to the implement of more restrict traffic rules, so is the marketing system.

Cultural Relics for Sale

The Chinese will sell anything. Since I've been here, I've visited several antique shops. Because of the lack of regulation and limited ability of the government to preserve historical artifacts, folks like me can sometimes find and purchase real cultural relics. However, there are also plenty of fakes. I almost bought an old clock at one shop, but my host told me it was not authentic.

Economic Information

Non-Public Economy

Although the public economy is still the main form of economy in China, there exist other forms such as private enterprises, foreign-funded enterprises, foreign enterprises and foreign individuals. The multiple economies provide more job opportunities, make a variety of products, and offer convenience to improve the lives of people. Therefore, the government is always encouraging and supporting the non-public economy. The rate of the non-public economy has grown quickly in recent years, and the non-public economy has become an important force in supporting the high-speed growth of the national economy. As in the following graph, the percentage of non-public gross industrial output value has risen quickly since 1993.

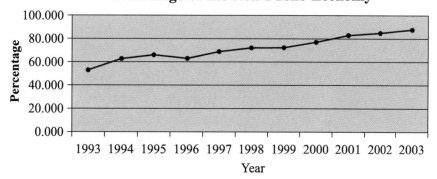

Percentage of the Non-Public Economy

As for foreign investment in China, there are various forms of investment in the country, such as Sino-foreign joint ventures, Sino-foreign cooperative ventures, foreign enterprises, BCT (Build-Cooperation-Transfer) investment, compensation trade, processing and assembly processing of materials imported and international leases. As a result, investors have more and more investment forms to select.

第八课 签 约
Lesson 8 Signing the Contract

Dialogue 1 Contract Draft 合同草案

一、合同草案

中方经理：史先生，根据我们上次的洽谈，我方准备了
一份合同。这是合同草案。

大　卫：有英文本吗？

中方经理：有，中文本和英文本都有，请您过目。不妥
之处我们可以再商谈。

大　卫：嗯，这个草案写得很清楚。但是，我想有的
细节还需要修改一下。比如，如果一方违约
的话……

中方经理：这一点我们考虑过。如果一方未执行合同，
那么另一方就有权终止合同，并有权索赔。

大　卫：我同意。我们应该把这个条款加进合同。

中方经理：好。我们会起草这个条款，然后再跟贵公司
讨论。

大　卫：谢谢。希望我们的合同能够早日签字生效。

Pinyin

Duìhuà I   Hétong Cǎo'àn

Zhōngfāng jīnglǐ： Shǐ xiānsheng, gēnjù wǒmen shàngcì de qiàtán, wǒfāng zhǔnbèile yí fèn hétong. Zhè shì hétong cǎo'àn.

Dàwèi： Yǒu Yīngwénběn ma?

Zhōngfāng jīnglǐ： Yǒu, Zhōngwénběn hé Yīngwénběn dōu yǒu. Qǐng nín guòmù, bù tuǒ zhī chù wǒmen kěyǐ zài shāngtán.

Dàwèi： Ēn, zhège cǎo'àn xiě de hěn qīngchu. Dànshì, wǒ xiǎng yǒude xìjié hái xūyào xiūgǎi yíxià. Bǐrú, rúguǒ yìfāng wéiyuē dehuà……

Zhōngfāng jīnglǐ： Zhè yìdiǎn wǒmen kǎolǜguo. Rúguǒ yìfāng wèi zhíxíng hétong, nàme lìngyìfāng jiù yǒuquán zhōngzhǐ hétong, bìng yǒuquán suǒpéi.

Dàwèi： Wǒ tóngyì. Wǒmen yīnggāi bǎ zhège tiáokuǎn jiājìn hétong.

Zhōngfāng jīnglǐ： Hǎo. Wǒmen huì qǐcǎo zhège tiáokuǎn, ránhòu zài gēn guìgōngsī tǎolùn.

Dàwèi： Xièxie. Xīwàng wǒmen de hétong nénggòu zǎorì qiānzì shēngxiào.

一、合同草案

中方經理：史先生，根據我們上次的洽談，我方準備了
一份合同。這是合同草案。

大　衛：有英文本嗎？

中方經理：有，中文本和英文本都有。請您過目。不妥
之處我們可以再商談。

大　衛：嗯，這個草案寫得很清楚。但是，我想有的
細節還需要修改一下。比如，如果一方違約
的話……

中方經理：這一點我們考慮過。如果一方未執行合同，
那麼另一方就有權終止合同，並有權索賠。

大　衛：我同意。我們應該把這個條款加進合同。

中方經理：好。我們會起草這個條款，然後再跟貴公司
討論。

大　衛：謝謝。希望我們的合同能夠早日簽字生效。

ENGLISH TEXT

Dialogue Ⅰ   Contract Draft

Chinese Manager: Mr. Smith, following our last meeting, our company prepared a contract. This is the draft.

David: Do you have an English version of the contract?

Chinese Manager: Yes, we have both Chinese and English versions. Please take a look at this. We can discuss the content further if there is anything you need to change.

David: The draft is well-written and very clear, but I think some of the details need to be revised. For example, what if one of the parties violates the agreement?

Chinese Manager: We thought about that already. If one party does not follow the agreement, the other party has the right to terminate the contract and ask for compensation.

David: I agree with you on that. We should add that wording to our contract.

Chinese Manager: OK. We will draft that section and discuss the content with your company.

David: Thank you. I hope our contract will be signed and take effect soon.

Notes

▶ Grammar &Pattern Drills

1. 根据 (Prep.) "according to; in line with"

根据, followed by a noun or a gerund, often occurs before the subject to provide a basis or ground for an action.

根据 + N, Subj. + VP

Examples:

1. 根据合同，我们提出索赔。

   We demand indemnity in accordance with the contract.

2. 根据你们的报价，我们已经给贵公司电汇了五千美元。

   We have already wired US$5,000 to your company according to your quoted price.

根据 can also be used as a noun or a verb according to the context.

Examples:

3. 你们商品的价格有没有根据？(As a noun)

   Is there a basis for the price of your goods?

4. 我们的计划要根据市场的需要。(As a verb)

   Our plan has to be based on market demand.

Substitutive drills：

	合作计划，	我公司可以付广告费。
根据	王总裁的意见，	我们修改了合同。
	李小姐的记录，	美国公司同意减价百分之十。
	合同的规定，	我们有权索赔。

2. A 和 B + 都 + V "both A and B"

A and B are two "objects", placed before the verb phrase or before the subject and the verb phrase to be emphasized.

$$(Subj.) + A(和)B + (Subj.) + 都 + VP$$

Examples：

1. 美元和人民币我们都有。

   We have both US dollars and *Renminbi*.

2. 我们自由市场和国营商场都想去看看。

   We want to visit both free markets and state-owned markets.

Substitutive drills：

合同的英文本和中文本	王秘书		有。
中餐和西餐	大卫		想尝尝。
白酒和威士忌	宴席上	都	有。
国际贸易和国内贸易	这家公司		做。
工艺品和服装	这个小摊儿上		有。
英语汉语	玛丽		会讲。

3. 之 （P） *formal*

之，a classical particle，is often used between an attribute and the word it modifies in written Chinese or in a formal dialogue. There are mainly two ways to use 之：

（1） The meaning and usage of 之 is similar to those of 的.

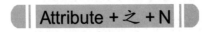

Attribute + 之 + N

Examples：

1. 我们洽谈之事已经写进了合同。

   The things that we discussed have already been written into the contract.

2. 这件新产品有很多与众不同之处。

   The new product is different from others in many ways.

(2) 之 can be inserted between a subject and a predicate, and change the structure into a noun phrase.

Subj. + 之 + Predicate = NP

Example：

3. 现在的生活水平之高，是几十年前无法想像的。

The living standard nowadays is so high that it was hard for people to imagine decades ago.

Substitutive drills：

合同		事，	我们明天再谈。
这种商品质量	之	高，	让批发商非常满意。
这家宾馆的服务		好，	让客人觉得像住在家里一样。
今天通讯技术		发达，	使人们在任何地方都能方便地联系。

There are some fixed forms that can only use 之 instead of 的，such as：

三分之一 （one third）

百分之五 （five percent）

问题之一 （one of the problems）

之所以 （the reason why...）

4. 如果……的话 (Conj. ...P) "if...; in case of"

如果 here is used as a conjunction to imply a supposition or a condition, 的话, which can be omitted, is usually placed at the end. The clause with 如果 is normally followed by another clause, with（那）……就 to show the conclusion or inference.

$$如果……（的话），（那）+ Subj. +（就）+ VP$$

Examples:

1. 如果你喜欢这个小古董（的话），我就送给你。

   If you like this small antique, I can give it to you as a gift.

2. 如果你们满意，那我们就成交了。

   We'll close the deal if you are satisfied.

如果 sometimes can be replaced by 如 in written Chinese.

Example:

3. 如有时间，请告知。

   Please let us know if you have time.

Substitutive drills:

如果	你们没有意见	（的话），	我们	就	签约吧。
	可以减价百分之十五		中方		同意订货。
	你喜欢这个工艺品		我		减价出售。
	你们公司想打开销路		我们		建立销售网。
	玛丽要到中国开洽谈会		公司		给她买机票。

5. ……过 （P） *used after a verb*

过，a particle，is used after a verb to indicate the completion of an action or an action once happened or a state once existed.

Subj. + V + 过 + NP

Examples：

1. 我和中方公司已经商谈过这件事了。(completion)

   I have already discussed this issue with the Chinese company.

2. 我去过北京的自由市场。(experience)

   I have been to the free market in Beijing before.

3. 这种服装在美国流行过。(a state once existed)

   This type of dress used to be popular in the USA.

Substitutive drills：

大卫和玛丽	都逛		中国的自由市场。
美方总裁	去		中国。
王小姐去年	翻译	过	这个合同。
美国公司跟中国公司	讨论		贸易合作的问题。
张董事还没有	看		会议的记录。

Supplementary Vocabulary

商务文件的常用词语
Common Words Used in Various Business Documents

表 17

English	Chinese	Pinyin
memo	备忘录	bèiwànglù
remarks	备注	bèizhù
catalogue of products	产品目录	chǎnpǐn mùlù
additional protocol	附加议定书	fùjiā yìdìngshū
appendix	附件	fùjiàn
purchasing contract	购买合同	gòumǎi hétong
labour contract	劳务合同	láowù hétong
selling contract	销售合同	xiāoshòu hétong
lease contract	租赁合同	zūlìn hétong
minutes（of a meeting）	会议记录	huìyì jìlù
deed；contract	契约	qìyuē
agreement	协议（书）	xiéyì（shū）

Dialogue 2　Official Contract Signing

<u>正式签字</u>

二、正式签字

总　裁：史先生，今天我们要签合同了。签字以前，不知贵方有没有要进一步商谈的事？

大　卫：作为美方公司的代表，我基本上同意合同中的各项条款，并感谢中方在价格上的让步。希望我们双方都严格执行合同。

总　裁：没问题。我们保证按照合同办事。我认为，不管哪一方违约，都有责任赔偿对方的损失。

大　卫：我举双手赞成。有关赔偿的金额和办法，已作为合同的附件加进去了。如果我们双方都没有不同意见的话，就可以签字了。

总　裁：好，这是合同的中文本和英文本，一式两份，请保存好。

大　卫：祝我们的合作圆满成功！

总　裁：是啊。好的开始，就是成功的一半。

Pinyin

Duìhuà II   Zhèngshì Qiānzì

Zǒngcái： Shǐ xiānsheng, jīntiān wǒmen yào qiān hétong le. Qiānzì yǐqián, bù zhī guìfāng yǒu méiyou yào jìnyíbù shāngtán de shì?

Dàwèi： Zuòwéi Měifāng gōngsī de dàibiǎo, wǒ jīběnshang tóngyì hétong zhōng de gè xiàng tiáokuǎn, bìng gǎnxiè Zhōngfāng zài jiàgé shang de ràngbù. Xīwàng wǒmen shuāngfāng dōu yángé zhíxíng hétong.

Zǒngcái： Méi wèntí. Wǒmen bǎozhèng ànzhào hétong bànshì. Wǒ rènwéi, bùguǎn nǎ yì fāng wéiyuē, dōu yǒu zérèn péicháng duìfāng de sǔnshī.

Dàwèi： Wǒ jǔ shuāngshǒu zànchéng. Yǒuguān péicháng de jīn'é hé bànfǎ, yǐ zuòwéi hétong de fùjiàn jiā jinqu le. Rúguǒ wǒmen shuāngfāng dōu méiyou bùtóng yìjiàn dehuà, jiù kěyǐ qiānzì le.

Zǒngcái： Hǎo, zhè shì hétong de Zhōngwénběn hé Yīngwén- běn, yí shì liǎng fèn, qǐng bǎocúnhǎo.

Dàwèi： Zhù wǒmen de hézuò yuánmǎn chénggōng!

Zǒngcái： Shì a. Hǎo de kāishǐ, jiù shì chénggōng de yíbàn.

二、 正式簽字

總　裁：史先生，今天我們要簽合同了。簽字以前，不
　　　　知貴方有沒有要進一步商談的事？

大　衛：作爲美方公司的代表，我基本上同意合同中的
　　　　各項條款，並感謝中方在價格上的讓步。希望
　　　　我們雙方都嚴格執行合同。

總　裁：沒問題。我們保証按照合同辦事。我認爲，不
　　　　管哪一方違約，都有責任賠償對方的損失。

大　衛：我舉雙手贊成。有關賠償的金額和辦法，已作
　　　　爲合同的附件加進去了。如果我們雙方都沒有
　　　　不同意見的話，就可以簽字了。

總　裁：好，這是合同的中文本和英文本，一式兩份，
　　　　請保存好。

大　衛：祝我們的合作圓滿成功！

總　裁：是啊。好的開始，就是成功的一半。

ENGLISH TEXT

Dialogue II   Official Contract Signing

CEO: Mr. Smith, we are going to sign the contract today. Before we do so, is there anything your company would like to discuss further?

David: As the representative of the US company, I basically agree with all the sections in the contract and also would like to thank your company for making a concession in terms of the price. I hope both parties can follow exactly what is outlined in the contract.

CEO: No problem. We promise to follow the contract. I feel whichever party violates the agreement has to assume responsibility and compensate the losses of the other party.

David: I totally agree with you. The amount and principles related to compensation have been added as appendices to the contract. If we both have no further disagreement on the contract, we can go ahead and sign.

CEO: OK, these are the Chinese and English versions of the contract, two copies of each. Please keep them.

David: I hope our partnership is satisfactory and successful!

CEO: Yes. Well begun is half done.

▶ Grammar &Pattern Drills

1. 不知 + A + not A "not know whether A or not A"

不知 here is followed by a "A + not + A" structure to introduce alternatives or uncertainty. It can form a question or a statement depending on the context. 不知 is similar to "do you know" when used to make a question.

$$(Subj.) + 不知 + A + not A$$

Examples：

1. 我们公司不知贵方同意不同意合作。

   Our company doesn't know if your company agrees to cooperate or not.

2. 李经理，不知这家宾馆有没有会议室？

   Manager Li，do you know if there are any meeting rooms in the hotel?

3. 李先生，我的意见不知对不对？

   Mr. Li，can you tell me if my idea is good or not?

Substitutive drills：

大卫		中方公司是否同意他的意见。
银行营业员		玛丽想不想开外汇账户。
检查人员	不知	张先生带没带违禁商品。
李小姐		在飞机上可不可以用笔记本电脑。
王经理		美方公司同不同意签字。

2. 作为 (Prep.) "as"

作为 can be used as a preposition to mean "in the capacity" or "in the role of". The phrase with 作为 can be placed either in front of the subject or after.

$$\text{Subj.} + 作为 + (\text{Subj.}) + \text{VP}$$

Examples：

1. 作为公司的总裁，你有责任执行这个合同。

   As the CEO of the company, you are responsible for executing this contract.

2. 我作为银行经理，可以帮您办理外汇存款手续。

   As the bank manager, I can help you to go through the procedure for foreign currency deposit.

作为 can also be used as a verb to mean "to take as" or "to regard as".

Example：

3. 大卫把张经理作为他的朋友。

David regards Manager Zhang as his friend.

Substitutive drills：

作为	公司的总裁助理，	大卫可以代表公司签字。
	翻译，	李小姐的汉语和英语都说得不错。
	国际银行，	我们可以为您提供全方位服务。
	财务主管，	李先生想听听董事们的意见。
	公司的总裁，	你应该保证按照规定办事。

3. 按照 （Prep.） "according to"

按照 here is used as a preposition to mean "in accordance with". This preposition is usually followed by a verb phrase and can also be placed before the subject.

Examples：

1. 我们按照合同索赔。

We claim indemnity in accordance with the contract.

2. 按照你们的意见，我们已经修改了有关条款。

We have already revised the items concerned according to your opinions.

Substitutive drills：

按照	合同，	我方提出索赔。
	讨论记录，	我们需要修改一下合同草案。
	李总裁的意见，	大卫要再跟中方公司讨论一下。
	你们公司的报价，	我公司同意进货。
	公司的规定，	我们不能减价。

4. 不管……都…… (Conj. + Adv.)　　"regardless of..."

不管……都……or 不管……也…… is usually used as a pair to indicate that the result will be the same in any case.

不管……，（Subj.）＋都/也……VP

Examples：

1. 不管贵不贵，他都要买这个古董。

   He will buy this antique no matter how expensive it is.

2. 不管怎样，我们都要满足买方的要求。

   We will satisfy buyers' demands no matter what happens.

The meaning of 不管 is similar to that of 无论 or 不论, however, 无论 or 不论 is usually used in written Chinese.

Substitutive drills：

不管	花多少钱，	大卫	都	要买这件工艺品。
	成功不成功，	玛丽		要去中国做生意。
	价格怎么样，	我们公司		要进这种商品。
	怎样处理，	我们		要让买方满意。
	你同意不同意，	公司		会这样做。

5. 有关 （Prep./ V/ Adj.） "in relation to；concerned"

The usage of 有关 here is similar to that of 关于. 有关 means "with regard to" or "concerning". However, 有关 can also be used as a preposition, a verb or an adjective.

$$有关 + NP, (Subj.) + VP$$

Examples：

1. 有关价格，我们可以再商量。（As a Prep.）
   Concerning the price, we can discuss it again.
2. 价格跟质量有关。（As a verb）
   The price is related to the quality.

3. 请你看一下有关文件。（As an adjective）

Please read the relevant documents.

Substitutive drills：

有关	这个问题， 签约的时间， 中文本合同草案， 自由市场的问题， 质量的问题，	我们 李总裁 我 我方	需要董事会讨论。 没有意见。 还没有过目。 可以给你介绍一下。 可以保证。

Supplementary Vocabulary

商务会议中的常用词语
Common Words in Business Meetings

表18

English	Chinese	*Pinyin*
propose；move	提议	tíyì
agenda	议程	yìchéng
speak（at a meeting）	发言	fā yán
consultation	咨询	zīxún
item on the agenda	议题	yìtí
adjourn	休会	xiū huì
objection；dissent	异议	yìyì
decide by vote	表决	biǎojué
vote	投票	tóu piào
second a motion	附议	fùyì
in favor of	赞成	zànchéng
vote down；veto	否决	fǒujué
passed；adopted unanimously	一致通过	yízhì tōngguò
motion；proposal	提案	tí'àn
chair of a meeting	主持人	zhǔchírén
abstain（from voting）	弃权	qì quán

David's Diary

Day 7: Signing the Contract

Translation

Today I met with my Chinese business partners. Based on discussion in our last meeting, they drafted a contract and presented it. I was impressed. They had two copies, one in English and one in Chinese. I've been told that any American doing business in China should only sign a contract that's translated. (I always want to be able to read the fine print.) After the meeting, I asked my host to compare the two contracts to be sure they both said the same thing. If I find out they are different, I will only sign the English version or wait until I can be sure they are both the same.

Binding

I'm surprised the Chinese are paying so much attention to the contract. I can tell they are concerned about our relationship and want to do business based on personal trust and respect, but they also want to have all the things we agreed to in writing. Now that China is interacting more and more with the West and becoming a global player, they are adopting some of the same standards of business we have in the USA.

Official Seals

Official documents in China always seem to have a seal. Sometimes they are made with red ink, similar to Chinese signature stamps known as "chops". I've also seen them use seals that make impressions on the paper, similar to notarizations in the USA. I wish I had brought an official looking rubber stamp with our company logo. That would have really impressed them. Next time I think I will.

Banquet

After we sign the contract, we will throw a party or a banquet for the Chinese businessmen at our hotel. My host told me this is a great way to seal the deal and honor our Chinese business partners. I'm letting my host choose the menu and will be taking cues from him all night to make sure I don't make any cultural faux pas.

Economic Information

China International Fair for Investment and Trade

The China International Fair for Investment and Trade (CIFIT) is the largest international fair in China, which is held by the Ministry of Commerce (MOFCOM) of China, and multiple relevant state ministries, commissions, offices, bureaus and associations are attended.

The CIFIT invites many foreign investors, traders, intermediate agencies, financial institutions, and representatives from foreign-funded investment companies. It is the best place for them to obtain the most up-to-date policies and information, investigate foreign projects, and evaluate the investment environment. The CIFIT is held each year from September 8th to 12th since 1997, and had been held successfully 8 times as of the end of 2004. In the eighth session, there were 118 countries and regions attending the Fair, with 11,841 business guests, signing 1,496 contracts, worth 14.9 billion USD. There were also agreements signed worth 10.19 billion USD. The volume of import and export trade reached 176 million USD.

In the 9th session, The CIFIT concentrated on property rights exchange and multinational purchase, matchmaking symposiums, trade and economic cooperation between the Chinese mainland and Taiwan.

第九课　参观工厂
Lesson 9　Visiting the Factory

Dialogue 1　Ordering Products │ 订货

一、订　货

厂　长：大卫先生，欢迎参观我们的工厂！

大　卫：谢谢。我早听说你们生产效率高，劳动力成本又低，生意特好。

厂　长：对。我们工厂原料充足，工人多，素质好，很有竞争力。

大　卫：你们今年的营业额如何？

厂　长：下半年的营业额高达八百万人民币。

大　卫：那你们的技术水平怎么样？

厂　长：我们的机器都是进口的，技术人员也是一流的，所以科技含量很高。

大　卫：如果我这个星期下订单，那什么时候可以提货呢？

厂　长：要看您的订单有多大，一般两三个星期就可以出货了。

大　卫：那付款方式呢？

厂　长：我们收现金、汇票，还有信用卡。

Pinyin

Duìhuà I Dìng Huò

Chǎngzhǎng: Dàwèi xiānsheng, huānyíng cānguān wǒmen de
gōngchǎng!

Dàwèi: Xièxiè. Wǒ zǎo tīngshuō nǐmen shēngchǎn xiàolǜ
gāo, láodònglì chéngběn yòu dī, shēngyi tè hǎo.

Chǎngzhǎng: Duì. Wǒmen gōngchǎng yuánliào chōngzú,
gōngrén duō, sùzhì hǎo, hěn yǒu jìngzhēnglì.

Dàwèi: Nǐmen jīnnián de yíngyè'é rúhé?

Chǎngzhǎng: Xià bàn nián de yíngyè'é gāodá bā bǎiwàn rén-
mínbì.

Dàwèi: Nà nǐmen de jìshù shuǐpíng zěnmeyàng?

Chǎngzhǎng: Wǒmen de jīqì dōu shì jìnkǒu de, jìshù rényuán yě
shì yīliú de, suǒyǐ kējì hánliàng hěn gāo.

Dàwèi: Rúguǒ wǒ zhège xīngqī xià dìngdān, nà shénme
shíhou kěyǐ tíhuò ne?

Chǎngzhǎng: Yào kàn nín de dìngdān yǒu duō dà, yìbān liǎng-
sān gè xīngqī jiù kěyǐ chūhuò le.

Dàwèi: Nà fùkuǎn fāngshì ne?

Chǎngzhǎng: Wǒmen shōu xiànjīn、huìpiào, háiyǒu xìnyòngkǎ.

一、訂　貨

廠長：大衛先生，歡迎參觀我們的工廠！

大衛：謝謝。我早聽説你們生產效率高，勞動力成本又低，生意特好。

廠長：對。我們工廠原料充足，工人多，素質好，很有競爭力。

大衛：你們今年的營業額如何？

廠長：下半年的營業額高達八百萬人民幣。

大衛：那你們的技術水平怎麼樣？

廠長：我們的機器都是進口的，技術人員也是一流的，所以科技含量很高。

大衛：如果我這個星期下訂單，那什麼時候可以提貨呢？

廠長：要看您的訂單有多大，一般兩三個星期就可以出貨了。

大衛：那付款方式呢？

廠長：我們收現金、匯票，還有信用卡。

ENGLISH TEXT

Dialogue Ⅰ　Ordering Products

Factory Director: David, welcome to our factory!

David: Thanks. I heard that your factory is famous for production efficiency and reasonable labor costs. Your factory does very good business.

Factory Director: Yes. Our factory has sufficient raw materials and lots of high-quality workers, providing us with a competitive edge.

David: What are the total sales for your factory this year?

Factory Director: The total sales for the second half of the year reached eight million *Renminbi*.

David: How is your technical competence?

Factory Director: Our machines are all imported. Our technicians are the best so our technical potential is very high.

David: If I place an order this week, when can I pick up the products?

Factory Director: It depends on how much you order. It usually takes two or three weeks to finish a job.

David: How about payment methods?

Factory Director: We take cash, money orders or credit cards.

Notes

▶ Grammar &Pattern Drills

1. 特 (Adv.) "especially"

特 is the colloquial form of 特别 when it is used as an adverb to mean "very" or "especially". However, 特别 can be used independently as an adjective, while 特 can't.

$$\boxed{\text{Subj. } + 特 + \text{Adj./ V}}$$

Examples：

1. 大卫在中国特忙。

   David has been very busy in China.

2. 他特了解市场。

   He knows the market very well.

Substitutive drills：

玛丽		喜欢高档货。
厂长要求	特	高。
这家商店生意		好。
工厂的原料		充足。

2. 如何 (Pron.) "how; what"

如何, a classical form of 怎么 or 怎么样, is used here to make a question.

Examples:

1. 订货如何办理?

   How to place an order?

2. 你们工厂的效率如何?

   How is your factory's production efficiency?

Substitutive drills:

请问,
| 你们的生意 | 如何? |
| 他们的技术水平 | |

| 你们想 | 如何 | 提高竞争力? |
| 你们打算 | | 付款? |

3. ……达…… (V) "reach; amount to"

达 can be used by itself or modified by an adjective to describe the measurement of length, capacity or weight. It is usually used in a situation which is considered amazing or unbelievable.

61

Subj. + (Adj.) + 达 + Num.

Examples：

1. 工厂的工人多达五百人。

   The factory has as many as 500 workers.

2. 这种车的速度可高达一小时一百二十英里。

   The speed of this car can be 120 miles per hour.

4. ……看…… (V) "depend on"

看，literally meaning "to see", is used here to express the meaning of "being decided by". It is usually modified by an adverb，such as 就，要 or 全，and must have an object.

Subj. + Adv. + 看 + Obj.

Examples：

1. 生产技术的高低得看技术人员的水平如何。

   The technical competence of the production depends on our technicians.

2. 能不能成交，要看厂长的意见。

   It depends on the factory director's opinion if we can make a deal or not.

Substitutive drills：

提货的时间	得		你们的订单有多大。
能不能签合同	就	看	总裁的意见了。
今年的利润如何	要		工厂的生产效率。
商店的营业额	全		你们的销售网了。

5. Approximate Numbers

Any two consecutive numbers from one to nine may be used to express approximation.

Examples：

一两年	（one or/to two years）
三四个星期	（three or/to four weeks）
两三千人	（two or/to three thousand people）
七八十美元	（seventy or/to eighty US dollars）

Supplementary Vocabulary

有关"税"的常用词语（续）
Common Expressions on Tax (continuation)

表 19

English	Chinese	*Pinyin*
business tax	营业税	yíngyèshuì
duty-free	免税	miǎn shuì
import/export duty	进/出口税	jìn/chūkǒushuì
property tax	房产税	fángchǎnshuì
stamp duty	印花税	yìnhuāshuì
surtax	附加税	fùjiāshuì
tax category	税种	shuìzhǒng
tax system	税制	shuìzhì
taxable items	税目	shuìmù
tax policy	税收政策	shuìshōu zhèngcè

Dialogue 2　Inspection

检　　验

二、检　验

厂　　长：真高兴有机会和你们合作。

玛　　丽：我们也是。你们工厂大，成本低，报价合理，出货也快，我们很满意。

厂　　长：谢谢。这里是成品，请您验收。

玛　　丽：很好。产品的质量不错，包装也符合国际标准。

厂　　长：这是报价表，请您先核对再签收。

玛　　丽：这价钱好像不对，比我们说好的贵了五千块！

厂　　长：上次大卫先生要求运货必须加保险，这五千块就是保险费。

玛　　丽：原来如此。保险费能不能便宜一点儿？

厂　　长：没办法，空运的保费比较贵。

玛　　丽：那海运的保费怎么样？

厂　　长：海运的保费只要一千块，但是慢多了。

玛　　丽：好，我向公司汇报一下，再作决定。

Pinyin

Duìhuà II   Jiǎnyàn

Chǎngzhǎng： Zhēn gāoxìng yǒu jīhuì hé nǐmen hézuò.

Mǎlì： Wǒmen yě shì. Nǐmen gōngchǎng dà, chéngběn dī, bàojià hélǐ, chūhuò yě kuài, wǒmen hěn mǎnyì.

Chǎngzhǎng： Xièxiè. Zhèli shì chéngpǐn, qǐng nín yànshōu.

Mǎlì： Hěn hǎo. Chǎnpǐn de zhìliàng búcuò, bāozhuāng yě fúhé guójì biāozhǔn.

Chǎngzhǎng： Zhè shì bàojiàbiǎo, qǐng nín xiān héduì zài qiānshōu.

Mǎlì： Zhè jiàqián hǎoxiàng bú duì, bǐ wǒmen shuōhǎo de guìle wǔ qiān kuài!

Chǎngzhǎng： Shàngcì Dàwèi xiānsheng yāoqiú yùnhuò bìxū jiā bǎoxiǎn, zhè wǔ qiān kuài jiù shì bǎoxiǎnfèi.

Mǎlì： Yuánlái rúcǐ. Bǎoxiǎnfèi néng bu néng piányi yìdiǎnr?

Chǎngzhǎng： Méi bànfǎ, kōngyùn de bǎofèi bǐjiào guì.

Mǎlì： Nà hǎiyùn de bǎofèi zěnmeyàng?

Chǎngzhǎng： Hǎiyùn de bǎofèi zhǐyào yì qiān kuài, dànshì màn duō le.

Mǎlì： Hǎo, wǒ xiàng gōngsī huìbào yíxià, zài zuò juédìng.

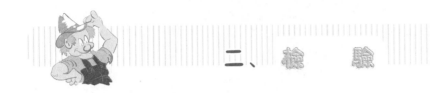

二、检　　验

廠　長：真高興有機會和你們合作。

瑪　麗：我們也是。你們工廠大，成本低，報價合理，出貨也快，我們很滿意。

廠　長：謝謝。這裏是成品，請您驗收。

瑪　麗：很好。產品的質量不錯，包裝也符合國際標準。

廠　長：這是報價表，請您先核對再簽收。

瑪　麗：這價錢好像不對，比我們說好的貴了五千塊！

廠　長：上次大衛先生要求運貨必須加保險，這五千塊就是保險費。

瑪　麗：原來如此。保險費能不能便宜一點兒？

廠　長：沒辦法，空運的保費比較貴。

瑪　麗：那海運的保費怎麼樣？

廠　長：海運的保費只要一千塊，但是慢多了。

瑪　麗：好，我向公司匯報一下，再作決定。

ENGLISH TEXT

Dialogue II Inspection

Factory Director: We are glad to have this opportunity to partner with your company.

Mary: We are also glad. Your factory is a big enterprise with low cost and reasonable price offering. Your factory is also very efficient. We are very satisfied with your performance.

Factory Director: Thank you. Here are the finished products. Please check them before acceptance.

Mary: Very good. The quality is not bad and the packing also meets international standards.

Factory Director: Here is the invoice. Please take a close look before you sign it.

Mary: The price seems wrong. It is five thousand dollars more than what we agreed to.

Factory Director: Last time David asked to add insurance to shipping. The five thousand dollars is the insurance fee.

Mary: I see. Can you make the insurance fee less?

Factory Director: There is nothing I can do about it. The insurance for air transport costs more.

Mary: How about the insurance for sea shipment?

Factory Director: It only costs about one thousand dollars, but sea shipment is a lot slower.

Mary: OK, I will have to report this to the company before we make a decision.

▶ Grammar &Pattern Drills

1. 你们工厂大，成本低 *topic sentence*

A Chinese sentence may contain a topic followed by a clause, and the clause may have its own subject and predicate. However, the topic of the sentence and the subject of the clause are usually related to each other. The relationship between the two is more like whole and part or super and subordinate, rather than possessive modification. The topic of the sentence appears at the begining, and the following clause functions as a comment describing the condition, state or situation of the preceding topic.

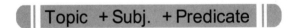

Topic ＋Subj. ＋Predicate

Examples：

1. 营业额今年很高。

   The volume of business is very high this year.

2. 工厂原料充足，技术水平却不太高。

   The raw materials in factories are sufficient, but the technical competence isn't high enough.

Substitutive drills：

今天	天气	不错。
我们工厂	机器	是进口的。
竞争力	这个公司	很强。
手工产品	中国的成本	很低。

2. 比 (Prep.) **"than"**

In addition to the usage introduced in Dialogue 1，Lesson 7，sometimes，比 can be used with a quantity complement indicating an actual amount or extent.

$$A + 比 + B + Adj.(了) + quantity\ complement$$

Examples：

1. 我们的成本比他们的成本多一百元。

   Our cost is one hundred dollars more than theirs.

2. 快信比平信快两天。

   Express mail is two days faster than regular mail.

Substitutive drills：

今年的营业额	去年	多	一百万。
用信用卡付账	用汇票	便宜	百分之一。
这里的包装费	那里	贵了	二十块。
飞机到达的时间	预定的	晚了	一个小时。

比

4. 慢多了　（Adj. + degree complement）　**"much slower"**

A degree complement is not always registered as an actual amount. It always appears after the adjective or verb it complements to show degree or extent.

$$\text{Subj.} + \text{Adj.} / \text{V} + （得） + \text{Complement}$$

Examples：

1. 这家工厂的生产效率低极了。

   The production efficiency is extremely low in this factory.

2. 海运比空运慢多了。

   Sea shipment is much slower than air transport.

Substitutive drills：

大卫最近	忙	极了。
这个小摊儿的生意	好	得很。
那家公司的技术水平	高	得多。
海运	慢	得不得了。

5. 向 (Prep.) "at; to"

向 here means "to" in the sense of "facing or toward someone or something". It is usually employed only when the action is dynamic. 向 can be placed before or after the verb phrase when it is used as a preposition.

$$\boxed{\text{Subj.} + 向 + \text{Obj.} + \text{VP}}$$

$$\boxed{\text{Subj.} + \text{VP} + 向 + \text{Obj.}}$$

Examples:

1. 经理向客人问好。

   The manager said hello to his guests.

2. 工人向厂长报告存在的问题。

   The workers report the existing problems to the factory director.

Substitutive drills:

公司	银行	借款。
你们可以	向	总裁	汇报。

资金	流	信息产业。
中国正在	走	向	现代化。

Supplementary Vocabulary

保险常用词语
Common Terms on Insurance

表 20

English	Chinese	*Pinyin*
insurance policy	保险单	bǎoxiǎndān
insurance premium	保险费	bǎoxiǎnfèi
insurance company	保险公司	bǎoxiǎn gōngsī
insurance contract	保险合同	bǎoxiǎn hétong
policy holder	保险客户	bǎoxiǎn kèhù
insurance period	保险期限	bǎoxiǎn qīxiàn
coverage	保险额	bǎoxiǎn'é
guarantee	担保人	dānbǎorén
home insurance	房屋保险	fángwū bǎoxiǎn
health insurance	健康保险	jiànkāng bǎoxiǎn
auto insurance	汽车保险	qìchē bǎoxiǎn
life insurance	人寿保险	rénshòu bǎoxiǎn
medical insurance	医疗保险	yīliáo bǎoxiǎn
dental insurance	牙医保险	yáyī bǎoxiǎn
buy insurance	投保	tóu bǎo

 人民保险
 太平洋安泰
 中华联合
 信诚人寿
 恒康天安
 金盛保险
 安联大众
 美亚保险
友邦保险

 华安保险
华泰保险
 中宏人寿
 天安保险
 泰康人寿
新华人寿
 太平洋
 中国平安
中国人寿

David's Diary

Day 8: Visiting the Factory

Labor and Equipment

Today I visited the factory, saw where the products will be made, and placed my first order. The environment was clean, the workers were wearing uniforms and the equipment looked state-of-the-art. The unskilled labor market in China is plentiful. And since the government is eager to attract foreign investment, tax incentives for anyone who starts a joint venture are tremendous. As a result, lots of new factories are springing up. Foreign businessmen have many choices, so the best factories have to be efficient and cost-effective in order to be competitive.

Methods of Payment

Paying for goods in China and having them shipped to the USA used to be difficult. Most Chinese companies needed to have a letter of credit from a US bank before they would ship. Now you can pay by credit card or money order. And of course cash is always accepted if you go there in person. However, the Chinese *yuan* is still nonconvertible, so it's a good idea to ask to be paid in US dollars when selling to China. A friend of mine who studied at a Chinese university in Beijing last year actually paid his tuition by credit card.

Shipping

I find most Chinese factories in Beijing like to ship by air when shipping internationally. Beijing has a new modern airport so it's perfectly suited for the task. However, I also find it's expensive—about 5 times as expensive as shipping by sea. But then there's the issue of getting products across land to a port city, like Shanghai, Guangzhou or Hong Kong. It also takes 2 to 3 months to ship something from China to the USA by sea. I think we will ship by air since it's so reliable and quick, but I have to make sure our profit margin is high enough to cover it.

Economic Information

Employment and Salary

With the development of China's economy, the employment and average salary have greatly increased in the last ten years. From 1994 to 2003, the employment in urban areas increased by about 39.2% and non-public sectors are becoming the major employers. Table 1 gives the detail information for employment.

Table 1   **Employment by Areas and Sectors**

	1994	1995	1996	1997	1998	1999	2000	2001	2002	2003
Urban Employed Persons (10,000)	18,413	19,093	19,815	20,207	20,678	21,014	23,151	23,940	24,780	25,639
State-Owned Units	11,214	11,261	11,244	11,044	9,058	8,572	8,102	7,640	7,163	6,876
Urban Collective-Owned Units	3,285	3,147	3,016	2,883	1,963	1,712	1,499	1,291	1,122	1,000
Cooperative Units	–	–	–	–	136	144	155	153	161	173
Joint Ownership Units	52	53	49	43	48	46	42	45	45	44
Limited Liability Corporations	–	–	–	–	484	603	687	841	1,083	1,261
Share-Holding Corporations Ltd.	292	317	363	468	410	420	457	483	538	592
Private Enterprises	332	485	620	750	973	1,053	1,268	1,527	1,999	2,545
Units with Funds from Hong Kong, Macao & Taiwan	211	272	265	281	294	306	310	326	367	409
Foreign-Funded Units	195	241	275	300	293	306	332	345	391	454
Self-Employed Individuals	1,225	1,560	1,709	1,919	2,259	2,414	2,136	2,131	2,269	2,377
Rural Employed Persons (10,000)	48,786	48,854	49,035	49,393	49,279	49,572	48,934	49,085	48,960	48,793
Township and Village Enterprises	12,017	12,862	13,508	9,158	12,537	12,704	12,820	13,086	13,288	13,573
Private Enterprises	316	471	551	600	737	969	1,139	1,187	1,411	1,754
Self-Employed Individuals	2,551	3,054	3,308	3,522	3,855	3,827	2,934	2,629	2,474	2,260

On the other side, the average annual growth rate of average salaries was about 23.3% from 1994 to 2003. Average wage in sectors is in Table 2.

Table 2　　　　　　　　　**Average Salary by Sectors** (unit: *yuan*)

	1994	1995	1996	1997	1998	1999	2000	2001	2002	2003
Average (a year)	4,538	5,500	6,210	6,470	7,479	8,346	9,371	10,870	12,422	14,040
State-Owned	4,797	5,628	6,280	6,747	7,668	8,543	9,552	11,178	12,869	14,577
Collective	3,248	3,931	4,302	4,512	5,331	5,774	6,262	6,867	7,667	8,678
Others	6,303	7,463	8,261	8,789	8,972	9,829	10,984	12,140	13,212	14,574

第十课　投　资
Lesson 10　Foreign Investment

Dialogue 1　Joint Ventures ｜ 合资经营

一、合资经营

总　裁：史先生，您看报了吗？又有一家美国公司要到
　　　　中国来投资了。

大　卫：听说了。这些年，中国的投资环境改善了，市
　　　　场大，回报高，吸引了不少外资。我们公司也
　　　　在考虑到中国投资。

总　裁：那太好了。中国加入世贸以后，我们公司正在
　　　　扩大国际市场，急需外资。如果你们买我们公
　　　　司的股份，我们可以合资经营。

大　卫：合资好是好，就是风险大。因为我们对中国的
　　　　投资政策不太了解。

总　裁：有时候，连我也不太清楚。特别是中国大陆和
　　　　台湾两岸同时入世，有很多新的问题需要研究，
　　　　也需要学习。

大　卫：活到老，学到老，对不对？
总　裁：一点儿也不错。

Pinyin

Duìhuà I Hézī Jīngyíng

Zǒngcái: Shǐ xiānsheng, nín kàn bào le ma? Yòu yǒu yì jiā Měiguó gōngsī yào dào Zhōngguó lái tóuzī le.

Dàwèi: Tīngshuō le. Zhè xiē nián, Zhōngguó de tóuzī huánjìng gǎishànle , shìchǎng dà, huíbào gāo, xīyǐnle bùshǎo wàizī, wǒmen gōngsī yě zài kǎolǜ dào Zhōngguó tóuzī.

Zǒngcái: Nà tài hǎo le. Zhōngguó jiārù Shìmào yǐhòu, wǒmen gōngsī zhèngzài kuòdà guójì shìchǎng, jí xū wàizī. Rúguǒ nǐmen mǎi wǒmen gōngsī de gǔfèn, wǒmen kěyǐ hézī jīngyíng.

Dàwèi: Hézī hǎo shì hǎo, jiùshì fēngxiǎn dà. Yīnwei wǒmen duì Zhōngguó de tóuzī zhèngcè bú tài liǎojiě.

Zǒngcái: Yǒushíhou, lián wǒ yě bú tài qīngchu. Tèbié shì Zhōngguó dàlù、Táiwān liǎng'àn tóngshí rùshì, yǒu hěn duō xīn de wèntí xūyào yánjiū, yě xūyào xuéxí.

Dàwèi: Huódào lǎo, xuédào lǎo, duì bu duì?

Zǒngcái: Yìdiǎnr yě búcuò .

一、合資經營

總　裁：史先生，您看報了嗎？又有一家美國公司要到中國來投資了。

大　衛：聽説了。這些年，中國的投資環境改善了，市場大，回報高，吸引了不少外資。我們公司也在考慮到中國投資。

總　裁：那太好了。中國加入世貿以后，我們公司正在擴大國際市場，急需外資。如果你們買我們公司的股份，我們可以合資經營。

大　衛：合資好是好，就是風險大。因爲我們對中國的投資政策不太了解。

總　裁：有時候，連我也不太清楚。特別是中國大陸和台灣兩岸同時入世，有很多新的問題需要研究，也需要學習。

大　衛：活到老，學到老，對不對？

總　裁：一點兒也不錯。

ENGLISH TEXT

Dialogue I   Joint Ventures

CEO: Mr. Smith, have you read the paper today? Here comes another American company to invest in China.

David: I heard about it. In recent years, China's investment environment has improved. China has a large market with high returns on investment, so it attracts a lot of foreign investors. Our company is thinking about coming to China to invest.

CEO: That is great! Since China joined the WTO, our company has expanded internationally, and we will really need foreign capital. If you buy shares of my company, we can have a joint venture.

David: It is good to have a joint venture, for sure, but fairly risky, because we do not have much knowledge regarding investment policies in China.

CEO: Even I myself don't know some of the policies. We have lots of new issues to explore, especially after both the mainland of China and Taiwan joining the WTO.

David: It's never too old to learn, right?

CEO: That is very true.

Notes

▶ Grammar &Pattern Drills

---

1. 正在/在 (Adv.) "in process of"

正在, an adverb, is always in the preverbal position to indicate an action in process. Sometimes，正在 can be replaced by 在.

呢，a final particle at the end of a sentence，can co-occur with 正在 in a sentence to emphasize the continuation of an action.

$$\boxed{\text{Subj.} + 正在/在 + \text{VP} + （呢）}$$

Examples：

1. 他们正在开会呢。

   They are having a meeting.

2. 我们正在讨论投资的问题。

   We are discussing the question on how to invest right now.

Substitutive drills：

服务生		工作	
玛丽		检验产品	
中美双方	正在/在	洽谈合同	（呢）。
小李		跟个体户讨价还价	

2. A 是 A，就是…… "It's A, to be sure, but..."

A 是 A here means concession which is similar to "although". The structure of A 是 A consists of two verb or adjective phrases with same key words. It is usually followed by 就是 or 可是.

$$\text{V/Adj.} + 是 + (\text{Adv.}) + \text{V/Adj.}, \text{就是/可是……}$$

Examples：

1. 保险费贵是贵，可是很有必要。

The insurance premium is high，yes，but it is very important.

2. 这个工厂大是很大，可是生产效率不高。

This factory is very large，all right，but the productivity is not high enough.

Substitutive drills：

坐出租车	方便		方便，		太贵了。
这家宾馆	贵		贵，		很舒服。
银行的利息	低	是	很低，	可是	比较安全。
你们的服装我们	满意		满意，		报价太高了。
这些产品	便宜		便宜，		质量不太好。

3. 对······V （Prep. ... +V） **"concerning..."**

Here，对 is a preposition followed by an object to form a prepositional phrase. The prepositional phrase indicates the concerning object of the verb.

Subj. + 对 + NP + V

Examples：

1. 大卫对这家中国公司很了解。

   David knows this Chinese company very well.

2. 李经理对台湾市场不太清楚。

   Manager Li doesn't understand the markets in Taiwan very well.

Substitutive drills：

王总裁		投资政策	很了解。
李厂长	对	产品质量	不太满意。
大卫		合同条款	很关心。
玛丽		中国古董	有兴趣。

4. 连······也······ （Prep. ... Adv.） **"even"**

Here，连 is used correlatively with 也 or 都 to emphasize. The noun after 连 can be either the subject，object or one other element of the sentence.

连 + NP + 也/都 + VP

Examples：

1. 连经理也不太了解国际贸易规则。

   Even the manager doesn't understand the rules on international trade.

2. 大卫连合同的细节都记得很清楚。

   David even remembers clearly the details of the contract.

Substitutive drills：

张小姐		复印纸		很节省。
因为忙，		睡觉		在公司。
为了多赚钱，	连	星期天	都/也	不休息。
马老板		领带		没打。

---

5. 一点儿……也不……   "one bit... was not..."

This pattern is to emphasize the meaning of "even", and it is always in the negative form. 也不 can be substituted by 也没 in this pattern.

Subj. + 一点儿 + 也不/没 + Adj./V

Examples：

1. 他一点儿也不了解中国经济。

   He doesn't understand the economy in China at all.

2. 这种商品一点儿也不好。

This product is not good at all.

If the verb in this pattern takes an object，the object is placed after 一点儿.

Example：

3. 李董事一点儿酒也不喝。

Trustee Li doesn't drink alcohol at all.

Substitutive drills：

	一点儿		也/都	
用信用卡				不麻烦。
我摊儿上的货，				不贵。
讨价还价，我				不会。
这家银行				不方便。
李经理		时间		没有。
玛丽刚到中国，		人民币		没有。
这位美国经理		汉语		听不懂。

中国的各类企业
Various Enterprises in China

表21

English	Chinese	*Pinyin*
single proprietary enterprise	独资企业	dúzī qǐyè
individual enterprise	个体企业	gètǐ qǐyè
factories, mines and other enterprises	工矿企业	gōngkuàng qǐyè
state enterprise	国营企业	guóyíng qǐyè
joint venture	合资企业	hézī qǐyè
transnational corporation	跨国公司	kuàguó gōngsī
business management	企业管理	qǐyè guǎnlǐ
enterprise group	企业集团	qǐyè jítuán
enterprise with foreign investment	三资企业	sānzī qǐyè
foreign-funded enterprise	外资企业	wàizī qǐyè

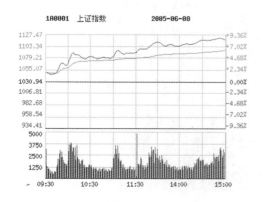

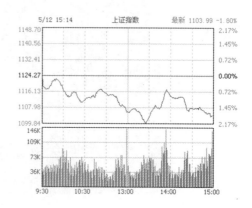

Dialogue 2　Stock Market Quotations

股市行情

二、股市行情

田经理：玛丽，你看，美国的存款利率又降低了。

玛　丽：是啊，为了刺激经济，美国今年已经降息好几次了。

田经理：那么，美国股市现在应该是买进的时候吧？

玛　丽：不见得。据有的经济学家估计，现在还是熊市，明年初牛市才来。最近中国的股市怎么样？

田经理：马马虎虎。上个月我以为中国的科技股看涨，所以加大了科技股的投资。可是刚买进就开始下跌，现在已经亏本了。

玛　丽：看来股东不好当啊。买股票有时就像赌博。

田经理：是啊，我想，买股票不如买债券，风险小。

玛　丽：我觉得如何投资得根据个人的经验。看来，你的投资经验越来越多了。

田经理：失败是成功之母嘛！

Pinyin

Duìhuà II　Gǔshì Hángqíng

Tián jīnglǐ：Mǎlì, nǐ kàn, Měiguó de cúnkuǎn lìlǜ yòu jiàngdī le.

Mǎlì：　　Shì a, wèile cìjī jīngjì, Měiguó jīnnián yǐjīng jiàngxī hǎo jǐ cì le.

Tián jīnglǐ：Nàme, Měiguó gǔshì xiànzài yīnggāi shì mǎijìn de shíhou ba?

Mǎlì：　　Bú jiàn de. Jù yǒude jīngjìxuéjiā gūjì, xiànzài háishi xióngshì, míngnián chū niúshì cái lái. Zuìjìn Zhōngguó de gǔshì zěnmeyàng?

Tián jīnglǐ：Mǎmahūhū. Shàng ge yuè wǒ yǐwéi Zhōngguó de kējìgǔ kànzhǎng, suǒyǐ jiādàle kējìgǔ de tóuzī. Kěshì gāng mǎijìn jiù kāishǐ xiàdiē, xiànzài yǐjīng kuīběn le.

Mǎlì：　　Kànlái gǔdōng bù hǎo dāng a. Mǎi gǔpiào yǒushí jiù xiàng dǔbó.

Tián jīnglǐ：Shì a, wǒ xiǎng, mǎi gǔpiào bùrú mǎi zhàiquàn, fēngxiǎn xiǎo.

Mǎlì：　　Wǒ juéde rúhé tóuzī děi gēnjù gèrén de jīngyàn. Kànlái, nǐ de tóuzī jīngyàn yuèláiyuè duō le.

Tián jīnglǐ：Shībài shì chénggōng zhī mǔ ma!

二、股市行情

田經理：瑪麗，你看，美國的存款利率又降低了。

瑪　麗：是啊，爲了刺激經濟，美國今年已經降息好幾次了。

田經理：那麼，美國股市現在應該是買進的時候吧？

瑪　麗：不見得。據有的經濟學家估計，現在還是熊市，明年初牛市才來。最近中國的股市怎麼樣？

田經理：馬馬虎虎。上個月我以爲中國的科技股看漲，所以加大了科技股的投資。可是剛買進就開始下跌，現在已經虧本了。

瑪　麗：看來股東不好當啊。買股票有時就像賭博。

田經理：是啊，我想，買股票不如買債券，風險小。

瑪　麗：我覺得如何投資得根據個人的經驗。看來，你的投資經驗越來越多了。

田經理：失敗是成功之母嘛！

ENGLISH TEXT

Dialogue II   Stock Market Quotations

Manager Tian: Look, Mary. The rate for savings accounts in America has decreased again.

Mary: Yes. In order to stimulate the economy, the USA has decreased interest rates several times.

Manager Tian: Then, it should be the time now to buy into the American stock market, right?

Mary: Not really. According to some economists, it hasn't hit the bottom yet. The market will not rise until early next year. How about China's stock market lately?

Manager Tian: So-so. Last month I thought technology stocks were rising so I increased my investment in them. However, they went down when I bought them, so I lost money.

Mary: It seems that it is no easy job to be a shareholder. Buying stocks is like gambling.

Manager Tian: Yeah, I think I would rather buy bonds than stocks. Buying bonds is less risky.

Mary: I think how to invest depends on an individual's situation. It seems you are getting more and more experienced in terms of investing.

Manager Tian: Failure is the mother of success!

Notes

Grammar &Pattern Drills

1. 又……了 (Adv. ... P) "again"

This pattern here means a same action happened again. 又, as an adverb, is placed before the verb. 了, at the end of the sentence, indicates the completion of an action or a change.

Subj. + 又 + VP + 了

Examples：

1. 中国的投资环境又有改善了。

   The investment environment in China has improved again.

2. 昨天，美方公司跟中方公司又讨论了一次合同草案。

   The American company discussed the draft of their contract with the Chinese company again yesterday.

Substitutive drills：

大卫		到中国去
玛丽		要兑换人民币
李小姐	又	给公司发电子邮件	了。
这些家具的价格		提
美国银行		降息

2. 为了…… (Prep.) "in order to..."

为了 is followed by an object to indicate a reason or a purpose for an action. The phrase of 为了 can be placed before or after the subject. Sometimes，为了 can be substituted by 为 without change in meaning.

为了 + Obj., Subj. + VP

Examples：

1. 为了到中国做生意，大卫努力学习中文。

   David studies Chinese very hard in order to go to China to do business.

2. 为了打开销路，我们要建立销售网。

   We need to build a sales network to find a good market.

Substitutive drills：

为了	收发电子邮件，	我带笔记本电脑去开会。
	存放贵重物品，	宾馆的房间里提供保险箱。
	提款方便，	大卫开了个活期账户。
	提高零售商的利润，	批发商同意减价。

3. 才 (Adv.) + V "not until"

才 is used here to give the sense of "later than expected". It is usually preceded by an expression of time.

Subj. + time expression + 才 + V

Examples：

1. 中国 2001 年才加入世贸。

China didn't join the World Trade Organization until 2001.

2. 美方代表要等公司总裁过目后才在合同草案上签字。

The American representative won't sign the contract until the CEO of his company has read the draft.

Substitutive drills：

大卫	明年		去台湾做生意。
玛丽	下星期		能给公司报价。
你们	要交款以后	才	可以提货。
我们	收到定金后		发货。
这个合同	修改以后		可以签字。

4. 刚……就…… （Adv. …Adv.） "no sooner … than…"

This pattern emphasizes one action taking place right after the preceding one only a short while ago. Both adverbs are followed by verb phrases. Please note，you have to follow the order of actions successively，which means the action happened first should be placed before the second one.

Subj.₁ + 刚 + VP + (Subj.₂) + 就 + VP

Examples：

1. 大卫刚到中国就考虑在中国投资。

   David is considering investing in China right after his arrival.

2. 利率刚降，股市就涨了。

   The stock market is going up right after the interest rate went lower a short while ago.

Substitutive drills：

中国	加入世贸，		大卫		到中国投资了。
股市	涨一点儿，		经理		收了。
张老板	刚	回北京，		就	收到了很多电子邮件。
李小姐	给公司发了电子邮件，		公司		给她回了一份传真。
公司	下订单，		工厂		给他们发货了。

5. A 不如 B (...V...)   "A isn't as ... as B"

不如 here is used for comparison of two items，and it means that A is not equal to B. Sometimes the thing to be compared is stated after B.

$$A + 不如 + B + (Adj.)$$

Examples：

1. 独资公司不如合资公司。

   Exclusive investment in an enterprise isn't as good as a joint venture.

2. 这个牌子的空调不如那个牌子的空调便宜，可是那个牌子的空调的质量不如这个牌子的好。

The air conditioners of this brand are not as cheap as those of that brand. However, the air conditioners of that brand are of better quality than those of this brand.

Substitutive drills：

三星级宾馆	四星级宾馆	舒服。
发传真	发电子邮件	方便。
活期存款的利息	定期的	高。
用现金	用信用卡	安全。
这条项链	那条	好看。
喝葡萄酒	喝白酒	来劲儿。

不如（between the first and second columns）

6. 越来越 "more and more..."

越, an adverb used in this fixed form, is often translated as "to be getting more and more". The word after 越来越 can be either an adjective or a verb. This pattern can only be used with one subject. 越来越 never precedes a noun or a noun phrase, since 越 is an adverb, unlike English phrase "the more..., the more..." which precedes nouns or pronouns.

Subj. + 越来越 + AP/VP

Examples：

1. 商品的质量越来越好。

   The quality of the products is getting better and better.

2. 他越来越想去中国做生意。

   He increasingly wants to do business in China.

Substitutive drills：

这家公司		大。
生产的成本		低。
订货的零售商		多。
大卫	越来越	喜欢国际贸易。
李总裁		注意股市。
海关的检查		严格。

Supplementary Vocabulary

股市常用词语
Common Terms in the Stock Market

表22

English	Chinese	*Pinyin*
bond market	债券市场	zhàiquàn shìchǎng
bear market	熊市	xióngshì
bull market	牛市	niúshì
dividend	股息	gǔxī
fund	基金	jījīn
mutual fund	合股投资基金	hégǔ tóuzī jījīn
stock	股票	gǔpiào
share list	股票行情表	gǔpiào hángqíngbiǎo
stock broker	股票经纪人	gǔpiào jīngjìrén
stock exchange	股票交易所	gǔpiào jiāoyìsuǒ
stock market	股票市场/股市	gǔpiào shìchǎng/gǔshì
stockholder	股票持有人	gǔpiào chíyǒurén
stock market quotations	股市行情	gǔshì hángqíng

David's Diary

Day 9: Investment in China

World Trade Organization (WTO)

This evening as I write in my journal, I'm thinking about all the changes China has gone through recently. Even though the rate has slowed, China's economy is still one of the fastest growing in the world. After about 10 years of petitioning, in the fall of 2001, China was finally admitted to the World Trade Organization (WTO). What it means to many Western countries like the USA is that they have access to Chinese markets—such as insurance and financial services—that had previously been protected by the Chinese government. It also means lower risk to investors like me since China will now be conducting trade according to international standards. What it means to the Chinese people is that they will be able to purchase foreign products (e.g. cars) at much lower prices since the Chinese government has dropped the import tariffs as one of the requirements for importation.

In talking with my host and other Chinese people who speak English, I find that they are very excited about China's being admitted to the WTO. They know that their country makes up nearly 25% of the world's population and they are very proud of Chinese history and culture and want to be recognized as a "world player". Furthermore, members of the new middle-class in China are anxious to spend money to improve their lifestyles.

The stock market in Shanghai is becoming more and more popular. Although it's very volatile, young Chinese entrepreneurs like to play the market to try and strike it rich. As soon as a new company goes public, its stock spikes and then levels off, similar to what happens with IPOs in the USA. The problem I see is the lack of infra-structure surrounding the Chinese stock market. With no SEC in China, the chance for insider trading and other forms of corruption make the risks of investing much more unpredictable and therefore less manageable.

Economic Information

Stock Market in China

By the end of 2004, China's listed companies had issued a total of 670. 5 billion shares in the markets and had raised a total of RMB 81. 1 billion. The total market capitalization was 37. 06 trillion, equivalent to 5. 1 times of 2004 GDP, the outstanding capitalization RMB 1,180. 5 billion, 16. 3% of GDP. China has developed a nationwide equity market with two stock exchanges located in Shanghai and Shenzhen. Two major exchange markets issue both A-share and B-share stocks to raise fund from domestic and international investors. The stock issued capital, stock market value and total value traded for two exchange markets are in the following tables.

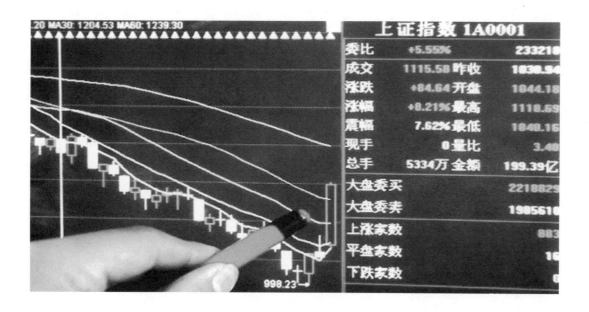

Table 1   Shanghai Stock Market

	stock issued capital	stock market value	total value traded
	0. 1 billion share	0. 1 billion *Yuan*	0. 1 billion *Yuan*
1997	975. 37	9,218. 06	13,763. 52
1998	1,280. 35	10,625. 9	12,386. 11
1999	1,580. 15	14,580. 47	16,965. 79
2000	2,032. 42	26,930. 86	31,373. 862
2001	3,164. 44	27,590. 56	22,709. 38
2002	3,727. 84	25,363. 72	16,959. 093
2003	4,170. 39	29,804. 92	20,824. 137
2004	4,700. 55	26,014. 34	26,470. 597

Table 2   Shenzhen Stock Market

	stock issued capital	stock market value	total value traded
	0. 1 billion share	0. 1 billion *Yuan*	0. 1 billion *Yuan*
1997	795. 86	8,311. 17	18,627. 88
1998	1,065. 01	8,879. 73	11,964. 97
1999	1,328. 70	11,890. 70	16,310. 86
2000	1,580. 97	21,160. 08	33,143. 78
2001	1,673. 91	15,931. 64	17,432. 48
2002	1,735. 15	12,965. 41	14,039. 68
2003	1,827. 54	12,652. 79	12,151. 60
2004	2,004. 47	11,041. 23	16,420. 53

第十一课 生意往来
Lesson 11 Business Connections

Dialogue 1 Public Relations 公关

一、公　关

厂　　长：这次美方下的订单数量很大，原料供应上可能有点短缺。

经　　理：这个我有门路。有几个厂商以前欠了我一点人情债，我跟他们谈一谈。

厂　　长：好，公关很重要。这次多亏其他厂商介绍，我们才能接到这笔大生意。

经　　理：我们也破例给了对方很优厚的回扣，还约定以后互相关照。

厂　　长：你看要不要去拜访一下这些厂商，顺便送个礼？

经　　理：也好。礼多人不怪嘛！

Pinyin

Duìhuà I   Gōngguān

Chǎngzhǎng: Zhècì Měifāng xià de dìngdān shùliàng hěn dà, yuánliào gōngyìng shang kěnéng yǒudiǎn duǎnquē.

Jīnglǐ: Zhège wǒ yǒu ménlù. Yǒu jǐ ge chǎngshāng yǐqián qiànle wǒ yìdiǎn rénqíngzhài, wǒ gēn tāmen tán yi tán.

Chǎngzhǎng: Hǎo, gōngguān hěn zhòngyào. Zhècì duōkuī qítā chǎngshāng jièshào, wǒmen cái néng jiēdào zhè bǐ dà shēngyi.

Jīnglǐ: Wǒmen yě pòlì gěile duìfāng hěn yōuhòu de huíkòu, hái yuēdìng yǐhòu hùxiāng guānzhào.

Chǎngzhǎng: Nǐ kàn yào bu yào qù bàifǎng yíxià zhèxiē chǎngshāng, shùnbiàn sòng ge lǐ?

Jīnglǐ: Yě hǎo. Lǐ duō rén bú guài ma!

一、公　關

廠　長：這次美方下的訂單數量很大，原料供應上可能
　　　　有點短缺。

經　理：這個我有門路。有幾個廠商以前欠了我一點人
　　　　情債，我跟他們談一談。

廠　長：好，公關很重要。這次多虧其他廠商介紹，我
　　　　們才能接到這筆大生意。

經　理：我們也破例給了對方很優厚的回扣，還約定以
　　　　後互相關照。

廠　長：你看要不要去拜訪一下這些廠商，順便送個禮？

經　理：也好。禮多人不怪嘛！

ENGLISH TEXT

Dialogue Ⅰ   Public Relations

Factory Owner: The order from the American company is huge this time. We might have a material shortage problem.

Manager: I know a way to solve the problem. Some suppliers owe me some favors. I will talk with them about supplying materials.

Factory Owner: Good . It is important to maintain good public relations in every aspect . Thanks to the recommendations of some other factory contractors, we were able to receive this huge order.

Manager: We also made an exception by giving them a high commission as well as agreeing to look after each other in the future.

Factory Owner: Do you think we need to visit these factory contractors and give some gifts out?

Manager: It sounds like a good idea. You can never go wrong with courtesies.

Notes

Grammar &Pattern Drills

1. 谈一谈 （∨—∨） **"talk about"**

Monosyllabic verbs can be used with 一 inserted in between. Reduplicated verbs, in general, have a less formal effect than those without them. They have two basic forms: monosyllabic reduplication and disyllabic reduplication. 一 and the repeated monosyllable verb usually take neutral tones. This form has basically two functions:

（1） To indicate an action of short duration.

Example:

1. 我得想一想。

   I have to think about it.

（2） To soften the tone and to make the speaker's tone less formal. This function is usually used in requests and suggestions.

Example:

2. 这个工厂值得看一看。

   This factory is worth visiting.

Subj.＋∨—∨＋(Obj.)

Substitutive drills：

请你	问一问	李厂长。
他想去自由市场	看一看。	
投资的事我得	想一想。	

2. 多亏 (V) "thanks to"

多亏 can be used as a verb with a clause or a noun as an object. It means a thing turns out as someone wishes with other people's help. Sometimes，多亏 can be followed by 了. 多亏 has no negative form.

Example：

多亏他开车送我，我才能准时到达。

Thanks to his driving, I arrived on time.

Substitutive drills：

今天	多亏（了）	大卫做翻译。
这次洽谈		李厂长。

多亏（了）	小王的介绍，	我才能有这份工作。
	你的信息，	我们厂才得到了订单。

3. 破例 （Adv.） "make an exception; break a rule"

破 means "break" and 例 means "rule" or "example". The action described after is an exception or something that rarely happens to the doer.

Examples：

1. 他破例给了小费。

   He broke the rule by giving the attendant tips.

2. 老板破例给他打了折。

   The boss made an exception by giving him a discount.

4. 互相 （Adv.） "each other; mutually"

互相 means either "A to B" or "B to A" is doing the same or has some relationships.

Subj. ＋互相＋VP

Examples：

1. 朋友应该互相帮忙。

   Friends should help each other.

2. 我们生意上互相照顾。

   We take care of each other's business.

Substitutive drills：

在合资公司里，中方和美方		协助。
在工作中，我们应该	互相	帮助。
两个公司的总裁		认识。

5. 顺便 (Adv.) "by the way；in someone's convenience"

As an adverb，顺便 is used in two situations：

（1）Taking the opportunity of doing A，one tries to do B at the same time without much extra effort.

Example：

1. 去中国旅行的时候，我顺便回老家看了看。

   While traveling in China，I went to visit my hometown.

（2）One is going to do A and someone else asks the one to do B for him at the same time.

Example：

2. 你出去的时候，请顺便把门关上。

   When you go out，please shut the door.

Subj. + 顺便 + VP

Substitutive drills：

去中国的时候，我要		去看看老朋友。
参观工厂以后，我们	顺便	逛了逛自由市场。
你去银行开账户的时候，		问问美元的牌价。

6. 怪 (V) "blame"

怪 is used as a verb here to mean "to blame". When used as an adjective, it means "odd" or "strange".

Examples：

1. 不是他的错，你不要怪他。(As a verb)

   It's not his fault. You shouldn't blame him.

2. 最近的股市有点怪。(As an adjective)

   The stock market has been quite odd recently.

Substitutive drills：

产品的质量不好，不能		推销员。
这次不能按期出货，要	怪	我。
如果这些产品没有竞争力，就要		我们的技术水平还不高。

Supplementary Vocabulary

广告业常用词语
Common Words in the Field of Advertisement

表 23

English	Chinese	Pinyin
advertisement	广告	guǎnggào
advertise	做广告	zuò guǎnggào
advertising agent	广告代理商	guǎnggào dàilǐshāng
advertising column	广告栏	guǎnggàolán
advertising fee	广告费	guǎnggàofèi
poster	广告画	guǎnggàohuà
commercial advertisement	商业广告	shāngyè guǎnggào
model	模特儿	mótèr
products on display	陈列商品	chénliè shāngpǐn
television advertisement	电视广告	diànshì guǎnggào
network advertisement	网络广告	wǎngluò guǎnggào

谁对路，谁就是新浪！

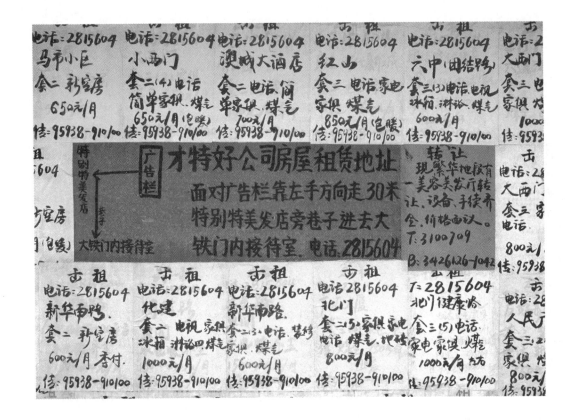

Dialogue 2　Building Connections

拉　关　系

二、拉关系

大　卫：听说中国人做生意很讲信用。

经　理：你说得一点儿都没错。不过要谈成生意，还得会拉关系。

大　卫：你是说有"关系"好办事吗？

经　理：是呀。在商务活动中，为了结识新朋友、建立合作关系，宴请是少不了的，尤其是近年来更加盛行。

大　卫：中国经济增长很快，我也想多投一些资。

经　理：我也许可以帮上忙，因为我认识一些业内人士。

大　卫：原来你也有"关系"啊！

Pinyin

Duìhuà Ⅱ Lā Guānxi

Dàwèi: Tīngshuō Zhōngguórén zuò shēngyi hěn jiǎng xìnyòng.

Jīnglǐ: Nǐ shuō de yìdiǎnr dōu méicuò. Búguò yào tánchéng

shēngyi, hái děi huì lā guānxi.

Dàwèi: Nǐ shì shuō yǒu "guānxi" hǎo bànshì ma?

Jīnglǐ: Shì ya. Zài shāngwù huódòng zhōng, wèile jiéshí xīn

péngyou, jiànlì hézuò guānxi, yànqǐng shì shǎo bu liǎo

de, yóuqí shì jìnniánlái gèngjiā shèngxíng.

Dàwèi: Zhōngguó jīngjì zēngzhǎng hěn kuài, wǒ yě xiǎng duō

tóu yìxiē zī.

Jīnglǐ: Wǒ yěxǔ kěyǐ bāng shang máng, yīnwei wǒ rènshi yìxiē

yènèi rénshì.

Dàwèi: Yuánlái nǐ yě yǒu "guānxi" a!

二、拉關係

大　　衛：聽說中國人做生意很講信用。

經　　理：你說得一點兒都沒錯。不過要談成生意，還得會拉關係。

大　　衛：你是說有"關係"好辦事嗎？

經　　理：是呀。在商務活動中，爲了結識新朋友、建立合作關係，宴請是少不了的，尤其是近年來更加盛行。

大　　衛：中國經濟增長很快，我也想多投一些資。

經　　理：我也許可以幫上忙，因爲我認識一些業內人士。

大　　衛：原來你也有"關係"啊！

ENGLISH TEXT

Dialogue II   Building Connections

David: I heard Chinese put lots of emphasis on keeping one's word when dealing with business.

Manager: You are absolutely right. However, in order to get the business done, you have to know how to build connections with people.

David: Are you talking about "connections", with which one can get things done easily?

Manager: Yes. In the business world, it is necessary to give a banquet to the business partners in order to get to know new friends and establish cooperative relations. This practice is getting more popular in recent years.

David: The economy in China has been growing rapidly. I would like to invest more.

Manager: I can help you with that, since I know someone in this field.

David: Oh, you also have your own "connections"!

▶ Grammar &Pattern Drills

1. 讲 (V) "pay attention to；stress"

讲，literally meaning "to say", is used here to express "stress". It can be modified by an adverb, such as 很, in this case. It can also be replaced by 讲究 (jiǎngjiu) in a more formal way.

$$\text{Subj.} + (\text{Adv.}) + 讲 + \text{Obj.}$$

Examples：

1. 他很讲人情。

    He is particular about people's sensibilities.

2. 商品要讲质量。

    We must stress the quality of the merchandise.

Substitutive drills：

这家公司	特别		效率。
做生意	尤其要	讲	信用。
服装	很		款式。

2. 不过 (Conj.) "but；however"

It is similar to 可是，often used in spoken Chinese. The meaning of 不

过, however, is softer than that of 可是.

Examples：

1. 我们工厂不大，不过生产技术很好。

   Our factory is not big, but our technology is very good.

2. 汉字很难写，不过很有意思。

   Chinese characters are very difficult to write, but they are very interesting.

Substitutive drills：

公关很重要，		要合法。
名牌货当然好，	不过	价钱贵。
海运慢是慢，		比较安全。

3. 尤其 （Adv.） "especially"

It has the similar meaning as 特别 when 特别 is used as an adverb. However，尤其 is often used in the second part of the sentence to point out the special one among others in the same category. 尤其 can be followed by 是 sometimes to make a phrase.

Examples：

1. 王先生对人很友善，尤其是对弱者。

   Mr. Wang is very friendly toward people, especially those who are weak in some way.

2. 我喜欢古董，尤其喜欢中国古董。

   I like antiques, especially Chinese antiques.

Substitutive drills：

中国经济增长很快，		加入世贸以后。
这个人很会办事，		会拉关系。
做事要讲信用，	尤其(是)	做生意。
我喜欢帮助别人，		帮助朋友。

4. 帮忙 (V) "help"

It is used in two ways：

（1）It can take an object or one other element. When it does，the object or the other element is inserted between 帮 and 忙. This usage is only for general help without specifying what the matter is. Sometimes qualifiers are used between the object and 忙.

Subj. + 帮 + Obj. + (qualifier) + 忙

Examples：

1. 我请他帮我个忙。

   I asked him to help me.

2. 李小姐帮了我很多忙。

   Miss Li has helped me a lot.

Substitutive drills：

请你		我一个	
李秘书能	帮	上你们的	忙。
这位厂商		了公司很多的	

（2）It is used to indicate a specific help and is usually followed by a verb phrase. In this usage, a noun phrase cannot be used after 帮忙.

| Subj. + 帮忙 + VP |

Examples：

3. 请你帮忙做会议记录。

   Please help record the meeting.

4. 你能不能帮忙来搬家?

   Can you come to help me move?

Substitutive drills：

你能不能		做广告?
他可以	帮忙	介绍客户。
李经理愿意		谈这笔生意。

Supplementary Vocabulary

中国反经济犯罪的常用词语

Common Expressions on Fighting against Economic Crimes in China

表24

English	Chinese	*Pinyin*
anti-corruption	反腐败	fǎn fǔbài
anti-corruption	反贪污	fǎn tānwū
anti-bribery	反贿赂	fǎn huìlù
anti-dumping	反倾销	fǎn qīngxiāo
anti-illegal copyright	反盗版	fǎn dàobǎn
anti-monopoly	反垄断	fǎn lǒngduàn
statute of fraud	反欺诈法	fǎnqīzhà fǎ
ban gambling	禁赌	jìn dǔ
ban (narcotic) drugs	禁毒	jìn dú
embargo	禁运	jìn yùn
building an honest and clean government	廉政建设	liánzhèng jiànshè
suppress smuggling	缉私	jī sī
wipe out pornography and other illegal publications	扫黄打非	sǎo huáng dǎ fēi

David's Diary

Day 10: Business Connections

Relations

As they say, it's not WHAT you know, but WHO you know. It's even truer in China than in America. Today, we had a bit of a problem with our Chinese partner. Our order was so big that they were concerned about their suppliers being able to fill it. Luckily, they built connections with other suppliers through the ones they've been dealing with. The term *guanxi* was used. I found out it literally means "relationship" and usually applies to one's relatives, but can also be extended to friends and business connections. There are pluses and minuses to *guanxi*. If you do someone a favor and they "owe" you, you can ask them to return the favor in the future and they are obligated to do so. This is great if you get in a pinch and really need help. If you don't want to be obligated to return someone's favor, you have to refuse his or her help.

Economic Information

China and the WTO

After 15 years of negotiations, China finally entered into the World Trade Organization (WTO) on Nov. 11, 2001. As the world's seventh largest trader, China's participation in the WTO will open a huge market and will be a boost for world trade.

China will definitely benefit from WTO membership in the long run, but the key to success will be the timing of reforms to the state-owned companies and financial services. Opening to the outside too early and too much will inevitably have a serious impact on the companies of China.

中国加入世界贸易组织签字仪式
SIGNING CEREMONY ON CHINA'S ACCESSION TO THE WTO
11 November 2001, Doha

第十二课 辞 行
Lesson 12 Saying Goodbye

Dialogue 1 On the Way to the Airport
去机场的路上

 一、去机场的路上

王经理：行李都准备好了吗？请上车吧！

大　卫：谢谢您亲自开车送我们。这次有机会和贵公司合作，真是太好了！

王经理：我们也很高兴和你们建立了生意上的往来。

玛　丽：商业交流提供了我们合作的基础。出货的事情要劳驾您了。

王经理：没问题。我们一定会按照合同准时出货。

大　卫：谢谢。等货一到，验收合格后，货款就会按期支付。

王经理：好的，我会和贵公司保持联系，确保一切按时进行。

玛　丽：希望我们合作成功，也祝贵公司生意兴隆，赚大钱！

王经理：谢谢。也祝您和大卫先生事事顺利！

大　卫：你们看，高速公路的下一个出口就是首都机场了。

Pinyin

Duìhuà I   Qù Jīchǎng de Lùshang

Wáng jīnglǐ: Xíngli dōu zhǔnbèihǎo le ma? Qǐng shàng chē ba!

Dàwèi: Xièxie nín qīnzì kāi chē sòng wǒmen. Zhècì yǒu
             jīhuì hé guìgōngsī hézuò, zhēn shì tài hǎo le!

Wáng jīnglǐ: Wǒmen yě hěn gāoxìng hé nǐmen jiànlìle shēngyi
             shang de wǎnglái.

Mǎlì: Shāngyè jiāoliú tígōngle wǒmen hézuò de jīchǔ.
             Chūhuò de shìqing yào láojià nín le.

Wáng jīnglǐ: Méi wèntí, wǒmen yídìng huì ànzhào hétong
             zhǔnshí chūhuò.

Dàwèi: Xièxie. Děng huò yí dào, yànshōu hégé hòu,
             huòkuǎn jiù huì ànqī zhīfù.

wáng jīnglǐ: Hǎo de, wǒ huì hé guìgōngsī bǎochí liánxì,
             quèbǎo yíqiè ànshí jìnxíng.

Mǎlì: Xīwàng wǒmen hézuò chénggōng, yě zhù guìgōngsī
             shēngyi xīnglóng, zhuàn dà qián!

Wáng jīnglǐ: Xièxie. Yě zhù nín hé Dàwèi xiānsheng shìshì
             shùnlì.

Dàwèi: Nǐmen kàn, gāosù gōnglù de xià yí ge chūkǒu jiù
             shì Shǒudū Jīchǎng le.

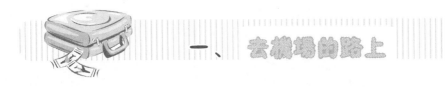

一、去機場的路上

王經理：行李都準備好了嗎？請上車吧！

大　　衛：謝謝您親自開車送我們。這次有機會和貴公司合作，真是太好了！

王經理：我們也很高興和你們建立了生意上的往來。

瑪　　麗：商業交流提供了我們合作的基礎。出貨的事情要勞駕您了。

王經理：沒問題。我們一定會按照合同準時出貨。

大　　衛：謝謝。等貨一到，驗收合格後，貨款就會按期支付。

王經理：好的，我會和貴公司保持聯繫，確保一切按時進行。

瑪　　麗：希望我們合作成功，也祝貴公司生意興隆，賺大錢！

王經理：謝謝。也祝您和大衛先生事事順利！

大　　衛：你們看，高速公路的下一個出口就是首都機場了。

ENGLISH TEXT

Dialogue I　On the Way to the Airport

Manager Wang:	Are you all packed and ready to go? Please get into the car.
David:	Thank you for taking us to the airport in person. It is great to have the opportunity to do business with your company.
Manager Wang:	We are also happy to establish business connections with you.
Mary:	Business exchange provides a foundation for partnership. Would you mind taking care of the shipping matter?
Manager Wang:	No problem. We will definitely ship the items according to the designated time in our contract.
David:	Thanks. Once we receive the items, we will inspect them. If the items are all satisfactory, the money will be paid on time.
Manager Wang:	OK. I will keep in touch with your company and make sure everything proceeds as planned.
Mary:	I hope our partnership will succeed. And I hope your business is booming and wish your company a good fortune.
Manager Wang:	Thanks. I also wish you and David good luck with everything.
David:	Look, the next exit on the highway is Beijing Capital Airport.

Notes

Grammar & Pattern Drills

1. 亲自 (Adv.) "in person"

亲自, an adverb placed before the verb, means "doing something by oneself". It is often used to show respect for a person holding a senior or higher position.

Subj. + 亲自 + VP

Examples：

1. 李总裁亲自修改了合同草案。

   CEO Li has revised the contract draft himself.

2. 王经理亲自去机场接玛丽。

   Manager Wang will go to the airport to pick up Mary himself.

Substitutive drills：

董事长		给客人点菜。
张厂长		带大卫去银行。
爸爸	亲自	给女儿准备行李。
王总裁		签收进口货物。
李老师		带学生去旅游。

2. 一……就…… "as soon as; no sooner... than"

一 and 就 are replaced before two different verbs to indicate one action taking place right after another one. The two verb phrases can share one subject or belong to different subjects. Please note, Action One after 一 happens before Action Two introduced by 就.

$$Subj. + 一 + V_1 + (Subj.) + 就 + V_2$$

Examples：

1. 大卫一到北京就给他的公司发了电子邮件。

   David sent an e-mail to his company as soon as he arrived in Beijing.

2. 中国一加入世贸，很多外国公司就到中国来投资了。

   No sooner has China joined the WTO than many foreign companies come to China to invest.

Substitutive drills：

大卫	起床，		到银行去办事。
玛丽	出机场，		兑换了五千元人民币。
李经理 —	到美国，	就	给公司发了传真。
财务主管	到，	我们	开会。
总裁	签字，	合同	生效了。

3. 按时 (Adv.) "on time"

按时 literally means "according to the time". 按 means "according to", and 时 means "time". It is always placed before the verb phrase, and "the time" is understood by both speakers and listeners. Sometimes, 按时 can be replaced by 按期. However, 按期 emphasizes "on schedule" rather than "on time".

Subj. + 按时 + V

Examples:

1. 洽谈会一定要按时召开。

   The negotiation meeting must begin on time.

2. 我们一定根据合同按时出货。

   We will certainly produce the goods on time according to the contract.

Substitutive drills:

去法国的飞机		起飞了。
大卫		来到国际贸易公司。
请贵方	按时	付款。
商业洽谈会		开始。
请各位旅客		登机。
我们一定会		付款。

4. 就是……了 "that is..."

就是 here is used correlatively with 了 to give force to the statement. A noun phrase is inserted between 就是 and 了. 了 indicates a new situation somehow.

Subj. + 就是 + NP + 了

Examples:

1. 明天就是签合同的时间了。

Tomorrow will be the time to sign the contract.

2. 看，前面就是自由市场了。

Look，the free market is in front of us.

Substitutive drills:

下星期		交款的时间	
高速公路的下个出口	就是	美国进出口贸易公司	了。
前面		中国银行	

就是了 can be used together as a phrase without insertion and placed at the end of a declarative sentence to mean "that's all" or reinfore the statement.

Examples：

3. 他认识很多厂商，只是不愿意拉关系就是了。

   He knows many businessmen，but he is not willing to use his connections，that's all.

4. 请放心，我们依法办事就是了。

   Don't worry. We will act according to law.

Supplementary Vocabulary

有关交通的常用词语
Common Terms on Transportation

表25

English	Chinese	Pinyin
airplane	飞机	fēijī
bicycle; bike	自行车	zìxíngchē
bus	公共汽车	gōnggòng qìchē
civil airplane	民航	mínháng
business class	商务舱	shāngwùcāng
economy class	经济舱	jīngjìcāng
first-class cabin	头等舱	tóuděngcāng
flight	航班	hángbān
long-distance bus	长途汽车	chángtú qìchē
motorcycle	摩托车	mótuōchē
overpass; motorway interchange	立交桥	lìjiāoqiáo
passenger ship	客轮	kèlún
pedicab; tricycle	三轮车	sānlúnchē
rickshaw(old)	人力车	rénlìchē
regular bus (service provided by a unit)	班车	bānchē
train	火车	huǒchē
sleeping berth	卧铺	wòpù
hard seats (on a train)	硬席	yìngxí
soft seats (on a train)	软席	ruǎnxí
subway; underground railway	地铁	dìtiě
taxi; cab	出租汽车	chūzūqìchē

Dialogue 2　See You Next Time

后会有期

二、后会有期

玛　丽：王经理，谢谢您送我们，也感谢贵公司的
　　　　热情招待。

王经理：哪里，哪里。

大　卫：请转达我们对总裁先生的谢意。

王经理：一定。希望你们这次中国之行有收获。

大　卫：收获大极了。除了谈生意，还有了女朋
　　　　友。（看玛丽）

玛　丽：（不好意思）谁是你女朋友呀？

大　卫：时候不早了，玛丽，我们该上飞机了。糟
　　　　糕，我的登机牌不见了！

王经理：别急，再找找，也许在口袋里呢！

大　卫：找到了，在我的公文包里。还没上飞机，
　　　　我的时差就开始了。

玛　丽：就是嘛！等回到美国，你可能连家都找不
　　　　到了！

王经理：再见了！祝你们旅途愉快！

大卫、玛丽：谢谢您！我们后会有期！

Pinyin

Duìhuà Ⅱ   Hòu Huì Yǒu Qī

Mǎlì: Wáng jīnglǐ, xièxie nín sòng wǒmen, yě gǎnxiè guì
               gōngsī de rèqíng zhāodài.

Wáng jīnglǐ: Nǎli, nǎli.

Dàwèi: Qǐng zhuǎndá wǒmen duì zǒngcái xiānsheng de
               xièyì.

Wáng jīnglǐ: Yídìng. Xīwàng nǐmen zhècì zhōngguó zhī xíng yǒu
               shōuhuò.

Dàwèi: Shōuhuò dà jí le, chúle tán shēngyi, hái yǒule
               nǚpéngyou. (kàn Mǎlì)

Mǎlì: (bù hǎo yìsi) Shuí shì nǐ nǚpéngyou ya?

Dàwèi: Shíhou bù zǎo le, Mǎlì, wǒmen gāi shàng fēijī le.
               Zāogāo, wǒ de dēngjīpái bú jiàn le!

Wáng jīnglǐ: Bié jí, zài zhǎozhao, yěxǔ zài kǒudài li ne!

Dàwèi: Zhǎodào le, zài wǒ de gōngwénbāo li. Hái méi
               shàng fēijī, wǒ de shíchā jiù kāishǐ le.

Mǎlì: Jiù shì ma! Děng huídào Měiguó, nǐ kěnéng lián
               jiā dōu zhǎo bu dào le!

Wáng jīnglǐ: Zàijiàn le! Zhù nǐmen lǚtú yúkuài!

Dàwèi、Mǎlì: Xièxie nín! Wǒmen hòu huì yǒu qī!

二、後會有期

瑪　麗：王經理，謝謝您送我們，也感謝貴公司的熱情招待。

王經理：哪裏，哪裏。

大　衛：請轉達我們對總裁先生的謝意。

王經理：一定。希望你們這次中國之行有收獲。

大　衛：收獲大極了。除了談生意，還有了女朋友。（看瑪麗）

瑪　麗：（不好意思）誰是你女朋友呀？

大　衛：時候不早了，瑪麗，我們該上飛機了。糟糕，我的登機牌不見了！

王經理：別急，再找找，也許在口袋裏呢！

大　衛：找到了，在我的公文包裏。還沒上飛機，我的時差就開始了。

瑪　麗：就是嘛！等回到美國，你可能連家都找不到了！

王經理：再見了！祝你們旅途愉快！

大衛、瑪麗：謝謝您！我們後會有期！

ENGLISH TEXT

Dialogue II   See You Next Time

Mary: Manager Wang, thanks for bringing us here. I would also like to thank your company for its hospitality.

Manager Wang: No problem. It was our pleasure.

David: Please extend our appreciation to your CEO.

Manager Wang: Sure. I hope you have gained valuable information from the trip to China.

David: I do have gained a lot. Besides getting business done, I also have gained a girlfriend. (Looking at Mary)

Mary: (Mary is blushing.) Who is your girlfriend?

David: It is about time to go, Mary. We should be boarding. Oh, no, my boarding pass is missing!

Manager Wang: Don't panic. Look closely. Maybe it is in your pocket.

David: I found it. It was in my briefcase. Jetlag is starting to kick in even though I have not boarded the plane.

Mary: Oh, yeah! I think you may not be able to find your home after you arrive in America!

Manager Wang: Bye-bye! Wish you both a pleasant journey!

David and Mary: Thank you! See you next time!

▶ Grammar &Pattern Drills

1. 转达 (V) "pass on... to..."

This pattern is used to mean "to pass on someone's message to somebody else".

$$(请) + 转达 + N_1 + 对 + N_2 + 的 + N_3$$

Examples:

1. 请转达我们公司对李总裁的谢意。

   Please pass on our company's gratitude to CEO Li.

2. 请转达史密斯先生对贵公司财务主管的问候。

   Please give Mr. Smith's regards to the CFO of your company.

Substitutive drills:

请转达	我公司	对	贵公司	的	祝贺。
	中方代表		美方经理		问候。
	我方工作人员		贵方经理		敬意。
	董事会		合作成功		祝愿。
	王先生		贵方		谢意。

2. ……极了 "extremely"

极了 is usually attached to a verb or an adjective and used at the end of a sentence to express "extreme". It is often used in colloquial Chinese.

Subj. + VP/AP + 极了

Examples：

1. 他们在中国的生意成功极了。

   Their business in China has been extremely successful.

2. 史密斯总裁对我们的合作满意极了。

   CEO Smith is extremely satisfied with our cooperation.

Substitutive drills：

我们公司的生意	兴隆	
他们对我们的招待	热情	
在商务中心办公	方便	极了。
那些手续	麻烦	
我们对这次洽谈	满意	

3. 除了……还/也…… "besides A also B"

In addition to the usage introduced in Dialogue 2，Lesson 2 and in this lesson，this sentence pattern can have two subjects or two topics sometimes.

If it has two subjects, the first one should appear after 除了。 It is used correlatively with 也 in this pattern to mean "there is someone else in addition to someone given".

$$除了 + Subj._1 + (以外), Subj._2 + 也 + VP$$

Examples：

1. 除了大卫，玛丽也投资股票。

   Besides David，Mary also invests in stocks.

2. 除了今天，明天也有个会。

   There is a meeting tomorrow in addition to today.

Substitutive drills：

除了		(以外)，		也	
	李先生		王先生		做这个生意。
	这家公司		那家公司		经营家具。
	财务主管		董事长		想跟外商谈一谈。
	李小姐		张秘书		做记录。
	英文		中文		很有用。
	宴请		我们		要送礼物。

4. 谁……呀？ "Who...?"

谁 can be used in a rhetorical question with 呀 at the end to emphasize a point —no answer is expected.

谁 + VP + (呀) ？

Examples：

1. 谁不知道中国发展快呀？

   Who doesn't know China has been developing quickly?

2. 谁做生意不想赚钱呀？

   Who doesn't want to earn money while doing business?

Substitutive drills：

	不愿意合作	
	是老外	
谁	不会讨价还价	呀？
	不想满足买方的要求	
	不愿意成交	

5. 还没/不······就······   "B happens even before A"

This pattern is used to emphasize that something happens even before the one that should take place ahead. 还 is followed by a negative statement in this pattern，and both 还 and 就 are adverbs followed by verb phrases. This sentence can have one or two subjects.

$$\text{Subj}_1 + 还没/不 + \text{VP}, (\text{Subj}_2) + 就 + \text{VP}$$

Examples：

1. 李经理还没学英语就开始跟美国商人做生意了。

   Manager Li started doing business with Americans even before he knew how to speak English.

2. 中国还没入世，史密斯先生就到中国来投资了。

   Mr. Smith had invested in China even before China joined the WTO.

Substitutive drills：

大卫	到香港		兑换了很多港币。
李小姐	到北京，		收到了北京公司的宴会邀请。
中国	入世，	外商	开始在中国做生意了。
王总裁 还没	到美国，	就	接到了美国贸易公司的订货单。
工厂	出货，	厂长	收到了订货公司的第一笔定金。
秘书	到，	会议	开始了。

Supplementary Vocabulary

辞行惜别的常用词语

Common Expressions to Your Business Partner Before His/Her Journey

表26

English	Chinese	Pinyin
take good care of yourself	多多保重	duōduō bǎozhòng
we'll meet again someday	后会有期	hòu huì yǒu qī
have a pleasant journey; bon voyage	旅途愉快	lǚtú yúkuài
win success immediately upon arrival	马到成功	mǎ dào chénggōng
may everything turn out as you wish	事事如意	shìshì rúyì
smooth sailing; may everything go smoothly	一帆风顺	yì fān fēng shùn
have a good and safe trip	一路平安	yílù píng'ān
may you be before the wind on your journey	一路顺风	yílù shùnfēng

David's Diary

Last Day：Saying Goodbye

The End is Only the Beginning

Today is my last day in Beijing and I feel sad. I have learned so much about Chinese culture, Chinese people and how to do business here. I now understand that relationships are important and so I will continue to keep in touch with my new business partners. This is only the beginning of a long and prosperous relationship that will hopefully benefit both sides.

I'm writing while waiting for my plane to depart at Beijing Capital Airport. I have noticed that Chinese say goodbye differently from Americans. They don't hug or cry or say a lot of words; they simply look deeply into their friend's or loved one's eyes and wave gently with one hand. I call it the "small goodbye", since it seems quiet and less fussy than an American goodbye. But I think the same sadness is felt and the same message—coming back soon—is communicated just as clearly, if not better. I know I plan to come back to China as soon as I can.

Economic Information

Tourism

China has become an important tourist destination in Asia, the fifth largest in the world. In 2003, the number of the tourists entering China reached 91.7 million, of which 11.4 million were foreign tourists, 54 times the figure for 1978. Consequently, the foreign exchange income from this industry reached US $17.4 billion, 67 times that of 1978.

In order to meet the need of the rapid development of tourism, China has built more and more travel agencies, hotels and restaurants. Similarly, China's transportation system, including railways, highways, water transport and civil aviation, has developed in a rapid way. Special trains and air-conditioned buses provide comfort and convenience for tourists. At hotels, tourists may book train, ship and air tickets to any destination.

China is rich in tourism resources. There are two major tour routes now. One is the traditional tour route, including historical sites, spectacular landscapes, and colorful and varied national customs like the Great Wall and the Temple of Heaven in Beijing. The other is the natural landscape tour route, like Mount Huang and Mount Tai. Chinese books, paintings, native products and rare-items shops can be found in most scenic spots.

Appendices 附录

Appendix 1: 中国改革开放大事记

Chronicle of Major Events in China's Reform and Opening Up

(1978 ~ 2004)

December, 1978. The 11th Central Committee of the Communist Party of China (CPC) made the decision to shift the focus of work toward modernization, and to carry out reform and opening up policies.

December, 1978. The heads of the 18 rural households in Xiaogang Village in Anhui's Fengyang County signed a contract to farm collective land on a family basis —the beginning of rural reform in the country.

July 15, 1979. The special economic zones were established in four cities— Shenzhen, Zhuhai and Shantou in Guangdong Province and Xiamen in Fujian Province. On May 16, 1980, the special zones were formally named special economic zones.

April, 1980. The first overseas-funded enterprise—Beijing Air Catering Co. , Ltd. was established in China.

August 18, 1980. The first special report on political reform—*Reform of the Party and State Leadership System* was made by Deng Xiaoping.

September 2, 1980. The State Council decided to enlarge its decision-making powers by all state-owned enterprises starting from 1981.

May 4, 1984. The CPC Central Committee decided to open 14 coastal cities to foreign investment.

October 4, 1984. The State Council endorsed and issued *Some Interim Regulations on Improving the Planning System* to subject economic activities to market regulation.

October 20, 1984. The 12th CPC Central Committee adopted *Decision of the CPC Central Committee on Reform of the Economic System*, with emphasis on reforms in cities.

January 1, 1985. The system of mandatory state purchasing for agricultural products was replaced by purchasing through prior contracts and purchasing on the open market.

February 18, 1985. The coastal economic development zones in the Yangtze River Delta, the Pearl River Delta and the Xiamen-Zhangzhou-Quanzhou area in southern Fujian were established.

March 13, 1985. *Decision on Reform of the Science and Technology System* was issued.

May 27, 1985. *Decision on Reform of the Educational System* was issued by the CPC Central Committee.

May 23 ~ June 6, 1985. The Central Military Commission decided to reform the military and downsize the People's Liberation Army by one million troops.

July 12, 1986. The State Council began reforming the labor-employment system with the application of the labor contract system.

December 5, 1986. The State Council decided to change the operation of state-owned enterprises, such as small state-owned enterprises could be leased and contracted on a trial basis.

October 25 ~ November 1, 1987. The 13th National Congress of the CPC adopted the strategy of modernizing China in three steps: the first step, ending in 1990, doubling the 1980 per capita GNP; the second step, ending in the year 2000, again doubling the 1990 per capita GNP; and the third step, by mid 21st century, China's per capita GNP will reach the level of the average developed countries.

April 13, 1988. China's largest special economic zone—Hainan Special Economic Zone (in Hainan Province) —was formally established.

September, 1988. The 13th CPC Central Committee approved in principle *Preliminary Scheme for Reform of Pricing and Wage Systems.*

June 23~24, 1989. Jiang Zemin was elected as General Secretary of the CPC Central Committee.

September, 1990. The CPC Central Committee and the State Council decided to develop the Pudong area in Shanghai.

December 19, 1990. The Shanghai Stock Exchange opened for business.

June 26, 1991. The State Council decided to gradually replace the old pension system that relied entirely on state enterprises for money.

July 3, 1991. The Shenzhen Stock Exchange opened for business.

January 18~February 21, 1992. Deng Xiaoping visited Wuchang, Shenzhen, Zhuhai and Shanghai on an inspection tour and spoke on his idea regarding the relationship between socialism and the market economy.

October 12~18, 1992. The 14th National Congress of the CPC decided that the goal of China's economic reform was to establish a socialist market economic system.

November, 1993. The CPC Central Committee adopted *Decision of the CPC Central Committee on Several Questions Concerning the Establishment of a Socialist Market Economic System.*

December 15 , 1993. The State Council decided to adopt a new system of financial administration characterized by tax revenue sharing between central and local governments.

December 25 , 1993. The State Council made a decision on reform of the financial system. The People's Bank of China was designated as the central bank charged with pursuing an independent monetary policy.

January 11 , 1994. The State Council made a decision on further deepening the reform of the country's foreign trade system.

February 19 , 1997. Deng Xiaoping, the chief architect of China's reform and opening-up programs, passed away.

September 12~18 , 1997. The CPC pointed out that realization of public ownership can and should take a variety of forms and that non-publicly-owned economic elements are important component parts of China's socialist market economy.

March 5~19 , 1998. The National People's Congress approved a restructuring program for the State Council, the central government, and cut the number of the State Council's component departments from 40 to 29.

1998~2001. The economic growth slowed down a bit after the 1980s. China's Growth Rate of GDP was 7. 8 in 1998, 7. 1 in 1999, 8. 0 in 2000, and 7. 5 in 2001.

December, 2002. The 16th National Representative Conference of the Communist Party of China held at the end of 2002, and it set up China's economic strategic target—the annual GNP target for the first two decades of the 21st century should be four times (two doubles) as much as the beginning of the century. If it happens, China's per capita will be over USD3,000, and China will transform from a lower mid-income to an upper mid-income country.

December, 2002. China's GDP reached 10. 2 thousand billion RMB.

Beginning of, 2003. China's central government in the State Development Plan put forward that the main tasks of economic development should be transformed to economic growth and improvement of employment. The China Banking Regulatory Commission was established.

January to June, 2003. China's economic growth rate was 9.9% in the first quarter of 2003. However, SARS epidemic attacked China in the second quarter.

Third quarter, 2003. China's economy returned to rapid growth after the anti-SARS war.

December, 2003. China's annual economic growth rate was 9.5%. China's per capita GDP was 1,094 USD. It was less than 200 USD in 1978.

December, 2004. China's annual economic growth rate kept stable at 9.5%.

Appendix 2 : Index of Supplementary Vocabulary

(Textbook Ⅰ & Ⅱ)

Acknowledgements

This business Chinese textbook series is one of the teaching material projects supported by the Chinese National Office for Teaching Chinese as a Foreign Language (NOTCFL). The office has been very encouraging in the implementation of this project we have undertaken. Our special thanks are due to Mr. Song Yongbo and Mr. Zhang Tonghui from the Department of Teaching and Research of the NOTCFL for their guidance and assistance. We are also very grateful to the editors of Beijing Language and Culture University Press for their valuable suggestions.

The chief editor of the textbook series is Dr. Xiaojun Wang, associated with Professor Zhang Wangxi and Professor Sun Dejin. Dr. Joy Huang, Ms. Linda Kuo and Ms. Cammy Chen made great contributions to the contents and exercises of this textbook series. Mr. David Silvey largely wrote the business and cultural notes while Ms. Yin Huiying, who also helped with the typing, provided most of the economic information. Mr. Alexander Donovan thoroughly proofread the English texts.

As teachers, we owe tremendous thanks to our students. We also owe our heartfelt thanks to our colleagues, especially to Dr. Timothy Light who kindly read the textbook and wrote the preface, to Dr. Cynthia Running-Johnson, and to numerous other colleagues for their inspirations.

The Authors

鸣　谢

本教材为中国国家对外汉语教学领导小组办公室规划教材。汉办对这一项目非常支持，教学处宋永波先生、张彤辉先生一直给予具体指导与协助。北京语言大学出版社的编辑为本教材提出了很好的修改意见，特此一并致谢。

本教材由王晓钧教授负责具体的编写工作，由张旺熹教授、孙德金教授共同策划审定。Joy Huang 博士、Linda Kuo Rice 女士和 Cammy Chen 女士协助编写课文和练习，David Silvey 先生主要撰写商业文化的比较，尹惠莹女士提供经贸信息部分并负责初稿的打字输入，Alexander Donovan 先生校读了全书的英文部分。

作为教师，我们要特别感谢我们的学生。我们也要衷心感谢黎天睦教授拨冗阅读全稿并为本教材作序，同时感谢 Cynthia Running-Johnson 博士等诸多同事的鼓励。

编者